A HISTO┣

TRURO

Looking back to the city from Garras Wharf,
near the start of Country Walk 3

First published 2003
by
LANDFALL PUBLICATIONS
Landfall, Penpol, Devoran, Truro, Cornwall TR3 6NR
Tel. 01872-862581

ISBN
1 873443 47 1

Typesetting, illustrations and maps by Bob Acton except where indicated.
The maps are based upon Ordnance Survey mapping
on behalf of The Controller of Her Majesty's Stationery Office.
© Crown Copyright. MC 100020399

Recent photographs are by Bob or Viv Acton unless otherwise stated.
The sources of all other illustrations are given where known,
but copyright ownership of a few has proved impossible to establish.

Printed by the Troutbeck Press
and bound by R.Booth Ltd., Antron Hill, Mabe, Penryn, Cornwall

Picture details
Front cover:
The western towers of Truro Cathedral as seen from High Cross.
The floral decorations are typical of the displays which over the years
have won many awards for the city.

Back cover:
Remains of a mid-19th-century gunpowder works in Idless Wood,
seen on Country Walk 1.

BOB ACTON

A HISTORY OF
TRURO

Volume 3
Exploring the City
- and Around

**Landfall Publications
2003**

Contrasting architectural styles on Old Bridge Street

CONTENTS

Acknowledgements

I am grateful to the following people for their various contributions to the contents of this book and/or their help with the research: Eric Berry (the Historic Buildings Consultant who is one of Carrick District Council's Conservation Officers) for taking my wife and me on a fascinating guided tour of Truro's most interesting buildings; John and Ann Pulford for providing the photograph of and detailed information about Scawswater Mill; Anthony Hitchens Unwin for the photograph of Coosebean Mill and factual summaries of the history of the various watermills on the routes; Dr James Whetter for information about Silvanus Trevail; and, as ever, John James for many photographs backed up with explanations.

The River Allen from the Moresk Road bridge, with the Moresk viaduct in the distance (Country Walk 1)

Introduction

Back in 1990 I was asked by a local shopkeeper to produce a small book featuring street maps of Truro and basic information about the city. I decided to add directions for five walks exploring points of historical interest, one focusing on the city itself and four country walks in the vicinity.

Thus was born *The Landfall Book of Truro*, out of print now. The present book is based upon it, but whereas the earlier one consisted of a mere 16 pages, now the City Centre Walkabout alone occupies 48. Even so, I have no doubt that readers familiar with Truro will detect many unfortunate omissions: inevitably so, since within the borders of the town are more than 300 buildings listed as being "of special architectural or historic interest" - far more than that, in fact, because several long rows of houses, such as the terraces on Daniell Street and at Ferris Town, are counted as single buildings for the purposes of the list.

Researching and writing this book has been an enjoyable experience, and I hope those who actually try the walks with book in hand will find it useful. Ideally they will also be encouraged by it to turn to the relevant pages of Volumes 1 and 2 for fuller detail and a better understanding of the historical context.

Bob Acton - May 2003

When exploring on foot the history of a town, it's always worth looking above the level of the shop windows.

*A view from the path between
St Clement and Malpas,
Country Walk 2*

*The River Allen as seen
from Old Bridge, on the
City Centre Walkabout*

*The Royal Hotel,
Lower Lemon Street,
which dates from
1799-1801*

A CITY CENTRE HISTORICAL WALKABOUT

About 2 miles

This is a figure-of-8 walk, in the sense that roughly half-way round it returns you to the start-point at the Cathedral: you could easily make two separate walks of it. The complete route is not lengthy, but Truro is a hilly city, and urban walking always seems to me much more tiring than its rural equivalent. Besides, as I hope to demonstrate, there are many points of interest that deserve to be lingered over, and it might well be more profitable to do just half the walk at a leisurely pace than to hurry round the whole of it. The second half of the figure-of-8 starts at section 6. The bold numbers at the starts of the sections correspond with the circled numbers on the street maps inside the front and back covers. The directions are picked out in bold type. Where more information or a relevant picture can be found in Volumes 1 or 2 of *A History of Truro*, the cross-reference is given in this form: (▶ Vol.1,53).

If you have a car to park and want to start and end the walk at the Cathedral, the most convenient car park is probably the High Cross multi-storey on St Clement Street; the Shoppers' Car Park on Old Bridge Street may be a little closer, but is "short-stay". As the street maps show, there is a good selection of other car parks close to other points on the route.

Sources of refreshments along the way are also plentiful, and there are public toilets at The Green bus station, at the bottom of Lemon Street (where it becomes Lower Lemon Street), in The Leats, at the Moorfield multi-storey car park (behind Mallett's) and at the Shoppers' Car Park.

The Cathedral stands on a site which was formerly occupied by the medieval parish church of St Mary, together with its churchyard and some neighbouring houses which stood on the north side. The south aisle of the old church was rebuilt and incorporated in the new building, and the small, copper-covered spire replaced the single spire of St Mary's. (The latter was added to the church in 1769; its pinnacle has been re-sited near Diocesan House, by Kenwyn Church: see Country Walk 1.) Designed by John Loughborough Pearson, the Cathedral was built between 1880 and 1910.

To deal adequately with the Cathedral's history and architectural features would be impossible in a book designed to be easily portable, and is hardly necessary in view of the easy availability of guide books and leaflets in the Cathedral itself (Tony Cartwright's *The Building and Ornamental Stones of Truro Cathedral* is particularly interesting), along with Canon H. Miles Brown's *The Story of Truro Cathedral* in the Tor Mark series. Best of all is

9

Fisher Barham's impressive photographic book, *The Making of a Cathedral* (Glasney Press, 1976), but copies are now hard to come by.

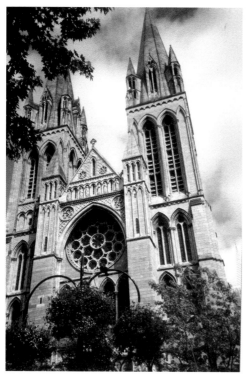

The central tower plus spire, almost 250 feet tall, commemorates Queen Victoria, who died two years before its completion in 1903; the two western towers and spires seen in the photo (204 feet, completed 1910) were dedicated to King Edward VII and Queen Alexandra. The exterior walls were built of dressed granite from the Carnsew Quarry at Mabe, with limestone from the Bath area used for details. Being much softer, the Bath stone was easier to carve, but unfortunately by the same token it has been severely eroded over the years. The statue of Charles I on the west front is a case in point: he has lost part of his head, a misfortune which adds insult to injury.

You may wish to identify the people represented. On the west front, the monarchs, from left to right, are Arthur, Alfred, George V, Charles I, Victoria (surprisingly positioned, facing north and therefore not always noticed), Edward VII, Alexandra, William I, Edward I, Henry V, Henry VIII and Elizabeth I. The bishops of Truro, at the lower level, are George Howard Wilkinson, Edward White Benson (our first bishop, later Archbishop of Canterbury), John Gott and Charles William Stubbs; finally, Archbishop Frederick Temple, who during his time as Bishop of Exeter worked for the creation of the Cornish see. Above the south porch are Humphrey Gilbert, Bevil Grenville, Canon "Tom" Phillpotts, J.L.Pearson (holding a plan of the Cathedral he designed: see page 34) and the Earl of Mount Edgcumbe. Canon Phillpotts (of Porthgwidden, Feock) gave the money for the porch, and is shown holding a model of it.

1 From the west front of the Cathedral, go towards Pydar Street.

Immediately right is Blewetts, which retains the classical façade of the Georgian Assembly Rooms (▶ Vol. 1,126-8), built to include a theatre in the late 1780s: look up to see a portrait of Shakespeare on the right; the other is generally said to be the actor David Garrick, but Nikolaus Pevsner states that it is Handel. Above them is represented a young lady - she is the Muse of Comedy, Thalia,

according to one good authority; the Roman Goddess of Wisdom, Minerva, according to another - holding a theatrical mask in her right hand and what looks like a mirror in her left - or is it a primitive tennis racquet? The Assembly Rooms provided a venue for events ranging from banquets, balls and music festivals to a performance in 1819 by "two wonderful Russian fireproof phenomena", one of them "eating a lighted torch with fork as if it were salad" (*Royal Cornwall Gazette*). The Assembly Rooms fell out of use as such when new Public Rooms were built on Quay Street, overlooking The Green, late in the 1860s. By the 1930s the High Cross building was, for a short time, the Delectable Duchy Tea & Cake Shop (▶ Vol.2,78-9) with the main central door providing access to the Cathedral Garage, in the yard behind.

Notice the water that (usually) flows along the gutters in the city-centre streets - a feature described in 1865 as "conducing to the general salubrity of the town". Leslie Douch's comment in his *Book of Truro* is that in those days the water "rejoined its parent river laden with organic filth". The dunghill that used to grace the end of St Mary's churchyard wall (roughly where the west front of the Cathedral now is) must have contributed generously to that (▶ Vol.1,180-4).

The name of the street that runs beside the square, High Cross, alludes to a cross that once stood here. The battered cross you see here now, raised on a tall column to match its name, is thought to be a thousand years old, and may well be the original one. It was found in a sewage trench under St Nicholas Street a few years back. During the 18th century (and probably before that) it was common practice to tether a bull to a ring attached to the cross so that it could be baited by dogs belonging to the tanners and fellmongers. In the early days it was in this square that Truro's Bullock and Beast Fair took place in November each year, and a monthly cattle market was held here from 1827 until it was moved to Castle Hill in 1840.

The building on the right at the corner with Pydar Street was Marks and Spencer's before the move to Lemon Quay in 2002. Before Marks, the site was occupied by the Post Office (built in 1885, demolished in 1974; photo on page 33 of Volume 2), one of 25 or more buildings in Truro designed or substantially modified by Silvanus Trevail (1851-1903). Sometimes described as "Truro's most famous architect", he was in fact born at Luxulyan, near St Austell, and some of his most important buildings are in other places, notably the Headland Hotel, Newquay, and a library in London (▶ Vol.2,33-4&47-8).

As you walk through the older streets it's usually worth looking up above the level of the shop fronts. A good example comes as you approach Pydar Street: opposite are the Cheltenham & Gloucester Building Society and ETS, in two contrasting old buildings: that on the left is brick-built and labelled

"Harvey", whilst the other, named "Burton", another Trevail design, sports a rather beautiful frieze (page 7). Harvey & Son described themselves as "Color and Glass Merchants" in Kelly's 1910 Directory; Burton's sold hardware.

Turn right into Pydar Street and walk as far as the side road on the right, Union Place.

Pydar Street was probably the first part of the town to be inhabited. It takes its name from one of the nine Hundreds into which Cornwall was divided for administrative purposes before the creation of urban and rural district councils. "Pydar", "Pyder" or "Pider" lay to the north of Truro, stretching from St Agnes to Padstow; Truro itself was in Powder hundred. Pydar Street, with its continuation, Kenwyn Road, is still one of the main links between Truro and places to the north; the distinguished Cornish historian Charles Henderson sees it historically as part of the important route between the Gannel and the Fal estuary. (For a little more about that, see the note about Idless in Country Walk 1.)

For a very short detour turn into Union Place.

The building now housing the City Library - originally the "Free Library and Central Technical Schools for Cornwall" - was one of many public buildings founded by J. Passmore Edwards (1823-1911), the son of a carpenter from Blackwater who made a fortune as owner of the *Echo*, the first halfpenny newspaper. The library's foundation stone, which he laid on 24 May 1895, is on the right side of the Pydar Street entrance; the Technical Schools section came a little later, and its foundation stone, dated 25 May 1897, is beside the entrance in Union Place. (The Technical Schools, at first co-educational, became a boys' secondary school in the 1930s, and continued as such till the opening of Truro's two comprehensive schools in 1979.) The architect was again Silvanus Trevail. Notice the dedication, above the door, to Sir Charles Lemon, great-grandson of the William Lemon who had Prince's House built and second son of Sir William, who oversaw the creation of Lemon Street. (More about both of these later.) Charles died nearly thirty years before the Central Technical Schools came into being, but the dedication is very fitting, since he had been a great champion of technical education, and was President and/or founder member of many learned bodies. Above the windows of the upper floor is a frieze (▶ Vol.2,48) depicting various arts, sciences and skills. Starting on the left, a painter, a sculptor and a musician can all be identified with reasonable confidence, as can a farmer and (a little further right) a scientist; the two men on the far right seem to be working an Archimedean screw - irrigating land in tropical climes, perhaps; the rest I'll leave you to puzzle over. (One gentleman appears to be carrying a roll of carpet...) Higher still is the coat of arms of the City of Truro (▶ Vol.1,11). It shows a ship and a fish (only one, though two are usually depicted), and is supported by a miner and a fisherman. The Biblical inscription, *Exaltatum cornu in Deo*, "Mine horn is exalted in the Lord", contains a hint of the "exaltation" of Truro to city status, and a punning allusion to "Cornubia", the ancient name for Cornwall. Plans recently announced by the City Council to sell off the Pydar Street end of the building in order to finance modernisation of the rest of the library have proved controversial, since many people feel that this would be contrary to the intentions of Passmore Edwards. The exterior of the library building has recently been sensitively repaired: the green paint, for example, is an exact match of the original, as discovered under many layers of other coats.

The right side of Union Place, opposite the library and technical schools, was occupied by the headquarters of the Royal Institution of Cornwall, along with the Museum, until it moved to River Street.

At the end of this part of Union Place is the neoclassical St Mary Clement Methodist Church (1830), now officially named simply Truro Methodist Church, following the closure of Truro's only other surviving Methodist church, St George's. Many prefer its unfussy dignity to the elaborations and show-iness of Trevail's edifice. Like many other notable buildings in Truro it was designed by the deaf-and-dumb architect Philip Sambell (1798-1874) (▶ Vol.1,177-8): hence the name of the coffee shop there. The interior fittings were remodelled by Trevail in 1885. It

provides an excellent venue for the annual competitive Cornwall Music Festival, and as a concert hall has advantages both visual and acoustic over the Cathedral.

Return to Pydar Street and continue as before.

The right side of the street was almost completely rebuilt during the 1970s, '80s and early '90s. The library is the only major exception. The frontage of what until February 2003 was Ottakar's Bookshop - it moved to Boscawen Street then - retains much of its 18th-century character as a miniature Palladian façade with central pediment, but everything behind it was demolished and rebuilt in 1992-3 (▶ Vol.2,222). The London Inn and other interesting old buildings used to stand on the sites now occupied by Boots and its neighbours.

The left side of Pydar Street has rather more of its original buildings, though transformed into shops and offices. No. 6 (currently Laura Ashley) retains its original early-18th-century ground-floor arches and sash windows;

next door (No. 7, the Orange shop), dates from about a century later, and still has its dressed ashlar masonry and authentic windows of that period.

Most interesting of all is the early19th-century shop front of what is now the Body Shop, very unusual in having its gable end facing the street. Above the shop window is a genuine 18th-century window. Towards the top end of the street are several early-19th-century houses now converted into shops and offices, and Solo Music's three-storey building dates from the 18th century.

Also on the left side are several narrow passageways, known locally as "opes" (pronounced "ops", and often called "opways"). Some of them are of fairly ancient origin, but all have been changed in recent years as a result of new building. One such is Pydar Mews, now attractively lined with small shops. You could go along that now, but I suggest instead that you continue a little further along Pydar Street.

2 Turn left immediately beyond the Halifax Building Society office.

This may seem at first to be another ope, but it soon widens into a little courtyard. On the right is a remarkable survival, a pair of 18th-century small houses plus a cottage, now occupied by the Pydar Gallery and the City Angling Centre. They are of stone and cob construction with original windows which open from the centre mullion rather than the side. In front is original cobbling, now very rare if not unique in Truro. Beyond, a sign spanning the way ahead announces "The People's Palace". Dating from 1906, the "Palace" started as a "club" for working men, offering many of the facilities of a pub, but without the alcohol. On or very near this site once stood one of Truro's many tanyards (▶ Vol.1,145).

When you get to the end, climb the short flight of steps* on the right; at the top turn left along Tregear Gardens, and at the T-junction turn right along The Leats. (* The gate at the top of the steps may possibly be locked; if so, my apologies for the fact that you will need to retrace your steps and get to The Leats via Pydar Mews or another ope.) "Tregear" or variants of it is a very common place name in Cornwall, "gear" deriving from the Cornish *ker*, a fort or round. Whether the use of the name here alludes to the nearby site of Truro's castle is uncertain: H.L.Douch points out that a man named Henry Tregeare lived in this district during the 17th century.

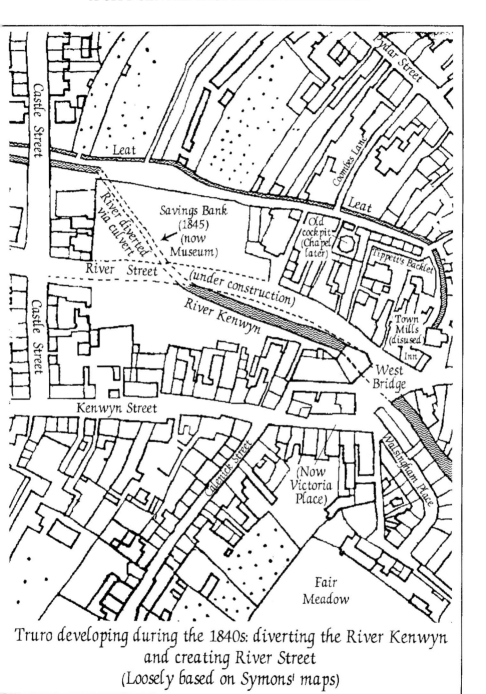

Truro developing during the 1840s: diverting the River Kenwyn and creating River Street
(Loosely based on Symons' maps)

A leat is an artificial watercourse. No leat is visible here now, but you will see a little later the leat, known as Tregear Water, which at this point runs beneath the road. This road, very useful for servicing the shops in Pydar Street, St Nicholas Street and River Street, was created in the late 1960s; till then it was only a narrow footpath running beside the open leat (▶ Vol.2,134). The leat brought water from the River Kenwyn to power the Town Mills (a triple grist mill which stood behind St Nicholas Street, close to what is now Victoria Square, until demolished during the 1840s), and also Mr Tippet (or Tippett)'s fulling mill, where woollen cloth was cleaned. It also was and still is - when not blocked or leaking - the source of the water in the town's gutters.

As you approach the road (Castle Street), notice the group of fine villas, their stucco painted a fairly uniform cream or mustardy yellow, on both sides - and there are several more on Frances Street, and at the lower end of Edward Street (page24), which you cross later. They date probably from the early 1830s, and most if not all are thought to have been designed by Philip Sambell.

The leat, and in the distance some of the villas

Cross Castle Street (with great care: look right for approaching traffic) and continue ahead along a path, with the leat on your right now and the River Kenwyn, deep in its man-made gorge, on your left. The "gorge" was dug, probably during the 1840s, to reduce the risk of floods and enable the river to be culverted under Edward Street and Castle Street. It was then diverted to the right (south), underneath what is now the County Museum, to flow on the south side of the then-new River Street. On Christmas Eve in 1999, 26-year-old Diane Hosking was lucky to survive when she fell into this river a little further upstream at Waterfall Gardens weir and was swept by floodwater through the tunnels under the streets, to emerge near the *Compton Castle* (on the far side of what is now the Lemon Quay Piazza), where two passers-by pulled her out.

Cross the next road, Edward Street (again with great care, this time looking left).

When it's safe to do so, look to your right, up Edward Street, to see the Courts of Justice, an award-winning building completed in 1988, where once Truro's medieval castle is believed to have stood. Its site was described as vacant as long ago as 1270. (▶ Vol.1,19-20) As mentioned earlier, Truro's cattle market was held there after 1840, but in 1983 it was moved to the outskirts of the City, on Newquay Road. The transfer of the County Court from Bodmin caused much controversy.

St George's Methodist Church and the River Kenwyn

After nearly 50m, where there is a footbridge over the leat, one option is to continue ahead. This would take you past the rear elevation of St George's Methodist Church, built in 1881, closed in 1996/7. On the left a little later are the attractive Waterfall Gardens, and you might care to walk through them to have a look at St George's Church and its neighbouring buildings, about which there is some information on pages 22-3.

Alternatively, cross the footbridge and pass through a wrought-iron gate into Victoria Gardens, opened in 1898 to commemorate the Queen's Diamond Jubilee. Here you have several paths to choose among: for

This photograph of the weir, sluice gate and viaduct dates from 1990.

example, the lowest continues close to the leat and river, enabling you to see the weir and the sluice gate which used to control the flow of water in the leat (it is now fed by a long pipe from another weir a little way upstream), while the highest passes beside a pretty bandstand.

Whichever way you select, keep heading generally north-west, towards the Carvedras railway viaduct, eventually passing beneath it. Notice the old stone piers (five remaining of the original thirteen) which supported the wooden superstructure of Brunel's 969ft-long viaduct, built in 1860. The all-masonry replacement was completed in 1902. (The name, Carvedras, has been interpreted as "Modred's round or fort"; H.L.Douch suggests that the Carvedras district once included the hill-top site occupied by an Iron Age fortification, where Truro's castle was eventually built.) **This brings you to Hendra Road,** whose name hints at the rural past (Cornish, *hendre*, home farm or ancient farmstead). Hendra farm is shown on Symons' map of 1848.

3 Turn left on Hendra Road and cross St George's Road, going very slightly right along the short side-road almost opposite, leading to the premises of Steve Andrews (Tyres) Ltd. On this site originally stood a medieval grist mill. It probably later ground corn for the Dominican Friary downstream in the Ferris Town area, which we reach soon on this walk route. By 1762 it comprised Carvedras Grist, Stamping Mills and Smelting House. The mill leat, beginning below Coosebean Mill (see Country Walk 4), still exists, and the two grist mills were still in use in 1817. For eight decades (from 1818 till closure in 1898) the Carvedras Smelting Works belonged to the Daubuz family; equipped with eight furnaces, it coined more blocks of tin than any other in Cornwall in 1835.

The Daubuz family was of Huguenot origin. Lewis Charles Daubuz Senior (1754-1839), was, writes D.B.Barton in *A History of Tin Mining and Smelting in Cornwall*, "the eminence grise behind Cornish tin smelting, his ability to command being aided because he 'so remarkably resembled the Duke of Wellington'." The family home until 1839 was the Mansion House at what is now called Daubuz's Moors, and their farm and garden there became one of the county's best-known nurseries, Treseder's. (See also page 54, and Country Walk 1, page 71.)

Turn left down the narrow George Street. As you go, notice the buttress on the right just past the entrance to Truro Motorcycles: the base of it, shown in the photo below, consists of a double tin mould. About 20m further on you

reach what was the main entrance to the smelting works. Although the building is now occupied by modern businesses, its external appearance is surprisingly little altered since a photograph of it was taken during the 1890s. (My sketch below is based on it. Notice the wooden superstructure of the old viaduct.) How much longer the building will retain its old shape remains to be seen: it has narrowly escaped demolition or drastic redevelopment at least twice in recent times. Late in 2002 planning permission was granted for conversion of the roof space into two flats; the roof is to be retiled with slate and the original louvred ridge vents, seen in the sketch, are to be reinstated. High up on the left side of the yard, "Arncliff" is the former count house (smelting works office).

Soon you pass St George's Church, built after a new parish was created from part of Kenwyn in 1846. Charles Henderson suggests that the dedication was prompted by a 15th-century chapel of St George which stood at the top of Chapel Hill. A wooden church was erected in 1849, to be replaced by this one in 1855. As seen from St George's Road, the church and its neighbours - "The Dorothy School" Sunday School building, the original vicarage (now

St George's Hotel Residential Care Home), and the early-19th-century
Carvedras House, which became the vicarage later - make an attractive group.
St George's, like St Paul's and St John's elsewhere in the City, is threatened
with closure: Truro is said by the Dean to be "over-churched" in comparison
with other Cornish towns.

As you walk on you may see a tall chimney in the distance ahead: I say
"may" because this belongs to the Royal Cornwall Infirmary, alias City
Hospital, which closed in 1999 - exactly 200 years since it was built - and
now awaits its fate. In October 2002 it was confirmed that plans have been
approved to build "a £6 million state of the art health centre" on the site.

Andrew Place, pictured below, is an attractive example of the kind of
terracing of small houses with round-arched doorways that was much more
common in Truro before the drastic post-war "slum clearance".

Continue till you reach the mini-roundabout, there turning left along Ferris Town, which takes its name from a local family who developed land here when the road was built. (They also owned at least two tanyards in Truro, including the one mentioned earlier, just off Pydar Street, and had Coronation Terrace built, opposite the railway station.) The name of the narrow street on the right, St Dominic Street, reflects the fact that a Dominican Friary was founded nearby in 1259, surviving until 1538 (▶ Vol.1,22). No trace of it remains. The attractive terraces around the junction of Ferris Town and Frances Street have in many cases retained their original iron railings, and their basement rooms are more typical of houses in bigger towns.

Bear right into Frances Street, which at the junction with Castle Street becomes River Street.

A short diversion along Little Castle Street, on the right, turning left into Kenwyn Street at the end, would show you several more surviving 19th-century shop fronts, such as the large corner premises with the "Redruth Brewery Company Limited" nameplates. On the right side of Kenwyn Street is a disused Wesleyan chapel, hard to recognise as such. It is now the Salvation Army headquarters, and can be seen through the rather ornate gateway beside No.13. Tucked in behind the former chapel is the last surviving British School building in Cornwall, now converted into residential accommodation. Dating from 1838 and designed by Sambell, it was identified only as recently as 2001.

23 Frances Street, with Rhondda House attached on the Edward Street side, is a good example of the kind of elegant early-19th-century villa of which there are several in this area. The porch is of a design peculiar to Cornwall.

River Street is aptly named, though there is no river to be seen: as explained earlier and shown on the Symons map, page 17, it flows under the road somewhere near the Museum entrance and then beneath the buildings on the right, and has been known to make its presence felt in the form of floods. The Royal Cornwall Museum is on the left. Its main building, designed by Philip Sambell, dates from 1845-7 and originally housed the Truro Savings Bank. From 1898 to 1908 it was used by Henderson's Mining School (▶ Vol.2,29-31), and in 1919 it was taken over by the Royal Institution of Cornwall, whose headquarters it still is. A little further along the street stands the former Baptist Church (1848-50, another of Philip Sambell's designs), annexed to the Museum during the 1980s.

Continue along River Street as it curves right before the corner with St Nicholas Street. This is one of the oldest streets in Truro: its name derives from the medieval guild called the Fraternity of St Nicholas, which owned houses here in the 13th century. On the right is Victoria Square, formerly known as Victoria Place. The culverted River Kenwyn flows beneath this, and, like River Street, it was an area much subject to flooding until very recent years. Until 1854 there was no "square": houses stood where there is now space for a few cars to park, but the houses were destroyed in a fire during that year. The River Street / St Nicholas Street junction is shown on old maps as West Bridge. No more than a footbridge beside a ford and stepping stones, it was the only bridge in the town over the River Kenwyn until the one at the bottom of Lemon Street was built in 1797-8.

This part of Victoria Square has not changed much since the 1950s, when this photo was taken. Mallett's, one of very few old-established retailers still trading i Truro, has taken over what was the Galleon restaurant, and Threshers sell wines next door, as R.M.Smeath did then. (Photo courtesy Robert Mallett)

4 Cross via the island at the junction with St Nicholas Street with due care and continue almost straight ahead along the narrow road on the left of the "Art Deco" main building of Mallett's store, Walsingham Place

(▶ Vol.1,176), a charm-ing little curved street of late Georgian terraces, complete with original windows and doors, with lion-head corbels sup-porting the flat hoods over the doors on the left. The stucco has been stripped from the houses on the right as you walk (left in the drawing) to reveal the rubble walls with brick dressings. Walsingham Place is still

one of the gems of Truro, despite the ugly Moorfield multi-storey car park that overshadows it. (Its saving grace is that it offers public toilets - at the top of a steps at the back of Mallett's and Somerfield.) The venerable-looking building on the left at the far end of Walsingham Place, now used as a store by Mallett's, began life early in the 19th century as a maltings; it still retains the little wooden turret which provided ventilation. Before Walsingham Place was built this was a marshy area known as "Caribee Island".

At the end, turn left and either walk through Lemon Street Market (if it is open when you do this walk *), turning right along Lemon Street when you emerge, or go on along Lemon Mews, beside the car park, and turn left at Charles Street, then right at the staggered crossroads. (* The market, established in 1978, was threatened with demolition as part of the ambitious "Opes" development scheme, but that has been abandoned, partly because Royston Leigh's redevelopment of Lemon Quay has gone ahead. In November 2002 the owner, Simon Hendra, unveiled new plans to replace the market with a two-storey building providing market stalls on the ground floor and an art gallery above. The old market closed at the end of January 2003, and demolition was well under way in April. The market site was formerly occupied by stables and a coach house, and an iron turntable for stagecoaches can still be seen near the Lemon Street entrance. The intention is that this and some other original features should be preserved in the new development.)

Continue up Lemon Street (▸ Vol.1,117-8). This, the most distinguished of Truro's thoroughfares, has been described as "the best Georgian street west of Bath". Despite a few modern intrusions, notably the cinema (built 1935-6) a little below the point where you have joined it, and the concrete-fronted building on the corner with Charles Street, it still provides a pleasingly harmonious spectacle, especially when viewed from the bottom of the hill. Most of the houses were built at the behest of

Sir William Lemon (1748-1824), grandson of the William Lemon who had Prince's House built. (More on that later.) The architect who oversaw most of the development was William Wood, who also designed the Royal Cornwall

Infirmary, the Royal Hotel in Lower Lemon Street, the Tregenna Castle Hotel in St Ives and Acton Castle, Perranuthnoe. Harmonious the houses may be, in both style and quality, but they are certainly not uniform, having been built over a period of some 35 years (1798 to the mid-1830s) by several builders using stone from several local sources. The granite paving slabs and kerbstones are a feature of the street.

The cupola of St John's Church, with another impressive villa next door

St John's Church, on the left, complete with Italianate cupola, dates from 1827-8. It was designed by Philip Sambell, and acted at first as a Chapel of Ease, but in 1865 a new parish to serve this part of the rapidly expanding town was created from Kenwyn. (In the same year St Paul's parish, whose church stands on Agar Road and overlooks Tregolls Road, was created from St Clement. As mentioned earlier in relation to St George's Church, all these three 19th-century churches face possible closure.) The wrought-iron gate on the left side of St John's is surmounted by an arch which incorporates some ancient-looking stonework; it has been suggested, though proof is lacking, that it may be a relic of the medieval Friary mentioned earlier. The official Listed Building description dates it to the 15th or 16th century. Whatever the truth may be, the doorway as a whole was brought across the road early in the 1960s from the St John's Sunday School building when that was demolished as part of the scheme for widening Infirmary Hill.

St John's Sunday School shortly before demolition
(Courtesy Western Morning News)

On the right, roughly opposite the church, are several impressive detached houses standing in their own grounds. Lemon House (which was The Deanery until its recent sale by the Church Commissioners) dates from 1815, Lemon Lodge from 1818, Southleigh House from 1833. Off Infirmary Hill is Mount Charles House, built in 1785.

Where the hill levels off slightly before continuing upwards is the Lander Monument (photo, page 102), on the left just before the junction with Barrack Lane. This name alludes to the fact that wooden army barracks stood here, in what was then a field called Fairmantle, between about 1804 and 1835 (▶ Vol.1,158). The monument commemorates the Lander brothers, Richard (1804-34) and John (1807-39), best known for their exploration of the River Niger (▶ Vol.1,168-70). It was originally intended as a memorial to Richard. The column, another of Philip Sambell's designs, was almost complete in May 1836 when it collapsed (probably through no fault of the architect's), and the extra cost entailed in rebuilding it led to a long delay before the statue itself could be commissioned. It was not until ten years after the death of John that the sculptor Neville Northy Burnard began work on the ten-foot-high, four-ton statue of Richard, which was finally placed on the 70-foot column in 1852. Unfortunately, the limestone Burnard chose has suffered badly since then, and both statue and column have had to be repaired more than once in recent years. (Burnard - born at Altarnun in 1818, died in Redruth Workhouse in 1878 - is a fascinating figure, whose life and works have been described by Mary Martin in *A Wayward Genius* [Lodenek Press, 1978]. See also Charles Causley's poem, "A Short Life of Nevil Northey Burnard". Causley's spelling of the name is the same as that used on the plaque erected at his birthplace in 1968. A bust of Richard Trevithick by Burnard is in the County Museum, River Street.)

Opposite the monument is the Daniell Arms, at the junction with Daniell Street. The name Daniell is closely associated with that of Lemon in Truro's history, as will be explained later; see also the information board on the left side of the pub entrance. All 49 terraced houses which line Daniell Street are listed, Grade II. They date from 1830. "Daniell Street," states Eric Berry, "has one of the best and most complete examples of early C19 planned terraces of small houses in the south-west."

Daniell Street. This photo was taken early in April 2003, immediately before the closure of the post office whose sign can be seen on the right.

(If you have the time and energy to walk further up the hill along the tree-lined Falmouth Road you will see one of the most attractive parts of the city, where very grand houses - now mostly divided into apartments or adapted as hotels or business premises - stand well back from the road. On the right is Truro High School, an independent school for girls founded - though not on this site - by Bishop Benson in 1880, the same year as its Methodist counterpart for boys, which will be seen later in the walk.)

5 **Now return downhill a few yards past the monument and turn right along Strangways Terrace**, yet another attractive example of the work of Philip Sambell. Its name derives from the maiden name of Sir Charles Lemon's wife. The building here began in 1837, when the barracks complex had been removed from the site. Notice the high pavement, intended to help the gentry mount and dismount their horses. The far end of the Terrace, near the pillar box, affords a good view over the city, dominated by the Cathedral and the Moresk railway viaduct; St Paul's Church, to the right, and Kenwyn Church, high up on the left, can also be seen, unless obscured by summer foliage. **Continue along Strangways Villas and take the sharp-left turning into Carclew Street**, with its long terraces of attractively varied cottages dating from the 1820s and '30s. ("Carclew" alludes to the Lemon family's country mansion, overlooking Restronguet Creek: see *Around the Fal*.) The turning on the right, William Street, features a chapel designed by Silvanus Trevail and built in 1883-7. Having ceased being used for worship in about 1960, it is now rather run-down and in use as a gym. Chapel Row, on the left further along Carclew Street, is dominated near the end by the rear of St John's Church.

Turn right on returning to Lemon Street. Watch, as you go, for attractive details such as the elegant doorway shown in the photograph.

Continue down past (on your right) Fairmantle Street and Lemon Quay/Back Quay. The building on the left opposite Lemon Quay, currently housing the Conservative Club and the House of Fabrics, was the home and office for many years of the architect Silvanus Trevail. (The commemorative plaque - which you may have some difficulty in finding! - was unveiled by Dr James Whetter, who has done much to call attention to the importance of Trevail's work.) Lemon Quay was developed soon after the building of a bridge over the River Kenwyn here, in 1797-8, in preparation for the construction of Lemon Street. The river, of course, still flows beneath the public toilets on your left and

the "piazza" on your right. The central part of the piazza used to be a car park dating from the mid-1930s, though some work on covering the river there had been done by the late '20s. (The walk runs along the north side of the piazza later - see section 6 of the directions, where a little more information is given about the history of this part of the town.)

Take the narrow passageway on the left, immediately beyond the toilets and the four K6-type telephone kiosks (listed buildings in their own right!).

Known as Roberts' Ope (referring to the old-established shop of that name which was, till June 2000, at the far end of it), the passageway runs beside the River Kenwyn for a few yards. From this point, in the distance can again be seen the tall chimney at the City Hospital - but see my comment on that on page 23. The little wooden turret with a weather vane on top is perched on the old maltings building, at the southern end of Walsingham Place (page 27). The ope next curves right and brings you to Boscawen Street, surfaced with granite setts.

Boscawen is the family name of Viscount Falmouth of Tregothnan, the owner of much property in the town from the mid-17th century until 1891, when most of it was sold. During that period the Boscawens probably exercised more influence on Truro's affairs than any other family. According to those who should know best (Lord Falmouth himself, for example!), the name is properly pronounced "B'zcawn".

The unusual width of the street is explained by the fact that it was originally two narrow lanes (Market Street and Fore Street) divided by Middle Row, the dilapidated buildings of which were demolished in the mid-1790s (▶ Vol.1,70). Middle Row consisted largely of shops, with the Market House at the west end (that is, the left end as you see it from Roberts' Ope) and a small prison at the east. (June Palmer in *Truro in the Seventeenth Century* refers to the fact that "any person found guilty of theft was liable to be flogged with thongs stuck to a stick right round Middle Row.") Like the later City Hall-cum-Market Hall, the old Market House - which survived till 1807 - doubled as Town Hall: the Council met on the upper floor.

Turn left along Boscawen Street, but after a few yards use the zebra crossing and turn right along King Street.

The Hong Kong & Shanghai Banking Corporation (formerly Midland Bank), on the right at the corner, occupies - along with Littlewoods - much of what was once the site of Lord Robartes' "Great House" - so called probably because of its height, four storeys (▶ Vol.1,64-5). It is thought to have been built about 1600, and parts of it survived until 1960. The Robartes family were the leading owners of property in central Truro during much of the 17th and 18th centuries, although Lanhydrock became their principal home during the 1620s.

Almost opposite HSBC is Barclays, an elaborate building in a very prominent position. Designed by the Redruth architect James Hicks, it dates from the late 1880s and was originally the premises of the West Cornwall Bank. Next door, in St Nicholas Street, the late-19th-century four-storey building which once housed Dingles department store and is currently occupied by Evans' clothes shop, is at least equally ornate: Eric Berry describes it as "Italianate style with early Gothic detail."

King Street's name dates only from the end of the 18th century (about the same time as other nearby streets were given regal or aristocratic names: Prince's, Duke and Boscawen). Earlier it had been called High Street; earlier still it was merely part of Pydar Street. Whilst the Market

House was at the southern end, much of the street would have been occupied by market stalls.

This soon returns you to the west front of the Cathedral.
6 To continue the full walk, or to start the second part of the figure-of-8, walk along the narrow street, High Cross, that runs beside the south side of the Cathedral.

As you pass the ornate South Porch of the Cathedral, look up to see the statue of John Loughborough Pearson, holding a plan of the building he designed.

The first passageway on the right is Pearson's Ope; like Roberts' Ope, it was named after one of the town's shops, in this case what was once Truro's leading jeweller's. **Take the second passageway on the right** - formerly Church Lane, but elevated to Cathedral Lane about a century ago. Notice the particularly fine granite paving here, with runnels on both sides. As you near the far end, I suggest you pause a moment to look back at the Cathedral: perhaps no view of it better illustrates the contrast between Truro Cathedral's setting and that of most of Britain's older cathedrals, insulated from their towns by their closes.

Cathedral Lane

On the right at the end of the lane is H. Samuel's jeweller's shop; look at its upper floors to see a good example of Edwardian mock-Tudor design incorporating unusual glazed white bricks. Dr James Whetter tells me that they were used because of complaints that the new building would take away too much light from its neighbours. The architect was Cornelius, who carried on the Trevail practice: Trevail had committed suicide in 1903, two years before this building was erected. (He shot himself in a ladies' lavatory aboard a railway train: for a detailed account of his life and especially his unhappy last three years, see Dr Whetter's article in the *Cornish Banner*, November 1993.)

The walk continues almost straight ahead, along Lower Lemon Street, but first it's worth going a few yards to your left. The Co-op "Pioneer" supermarket, on your left, stands on the site of "Mr Foote's Great House", which was built in 1671 and incorporated a Tudor courtyard (▶ Vol.1,132-4). In 1769 the Red Lion Inn, a couple of doors away, had fallen into disrepair, and John Foote's house was taken over as the new Red Lion. (The Foote family's main residence by that time was Pencalenick, near Tresillian; a descendant of John's, Samuel, became well-known as an actor and playwright in the 18th century (▶ Vol.1,126-7).) At that time the new inn was described as having "three very handsome parlours" and a dining room 73ft long, in addition to servants' accommodation and stabling behind. It was also noted for its beautiful staircase (▶ Vol.1,134). A new frontage was built in the late 17th or early 18th century, and Silvanus Trevail added two more floors in the Mock Tudor style late in the 19th. The Red Lion rivalled the King's Head (later called the Royal Hotel - see below) as a social centre and venue for business and public meetings. One of the blackest days in Truro's recent history was 14 July 1967, when a lorry descending Lemon Street ran out of control and smashed into the front of the Red Lion. What remained was pronounced unsafe and demolished, though the staircase was saved and taken to Godolphin House near Breage, where it remains in pieces, never having been re-erected. (A fuller account of what happened, and of the events leading up to the accident, is in Volume 2: see page 166.)

On the other side is the neoclassical façade of the City Hall, built in 1846-7 to combine market facilities and Municipal Buildings (▶ Vol.1,184-5). Council chamber, magistrates' court and other civic rooms are on the upper floor. Much of it became tatty and dilapidated in recent years, and several schemes for its refurbishment, adaptation or removal came and went, to the accompaniment of much lively controversy. Finally, the Boscawen Street side of the building was given a thorough wash-and-brush-up in the mid-1990s, at the same time as the Back Quay side and the former Market Hall were being transformed into the Hall for Cornwall: see below. Truro's Tourist Information Centre is on the ground floor on the Boscawen Street side, and on the right-hand wall of the rather grand but dark Boscawen Street entrance to the Hall is Jenkin Daniell's stone tablet, dating from 1615 and originally displayed in the old Market House. See Volume 1 page 66.

The City Hall (and part of Lemon Quay before the arrival of Marks & Spencer) as seen from the Cathedral's main tower (Photo by John James)

Proceed along Lower Lemon Street now, passing on your left Tony Price Sports. This strange example of "modern" architecture was built in 1963, when the old London House was occupied by WHSmith & Son (▶ Vol.2,158). On your right, Lloyds Bank is another Silvanus Trevail building in classical style - notice the small dome at the corner. The Royal Hotel (photo on page 8) dates from 1801. In that year, part of an old coaching inn called the King's Head had to be demolished so that the new Lemon Street could be linked with Boscawen Street, and this building was its replacement. It retained the original name till 1806, when it became Pearce's Hotel, having been bought by Mr W.Pearce from Redruth. For many years it played a leading part in the life of the town as a venue for such events as civic dinners, auctions, business meetings and balls, and in 1835 it was chosen for the lying in state of the body of Francis Basset, Baron de Dunstanville, en route for Tehidy. The hotel was still in the possession of the Pearce family in the 1850s, but by then it had been dignified with its present name: Prince Albert had been a guest there in 1846. Early in 1993 it was bought by Frank Manning, brother of the comedian Bernard: hence the name of the restaurant and bar.

Take the first left turning, Back Quay. The Market Inn (c. 1900), with its picturesque glazed tile and polychrome terracotta frontage, used to specialise in providing what was advertised as an "Irish Welcom"; no doubt the spelling, too, was Irish. In scale and style the pub - renamed the MI Bar and fully refurbished inside - contrasts violently with the imposing rear elevation of the City Hall, since November 1997 the main entrance of the Hall for Cornwall. (The long, tortuous story behind the creation of the Hall for Cornwall is told in Volume 2. Its roof and the fly tower above the stage can be seen in the photograph on page 37.) Further along, Woolworth's building dates from the mid-1950s, like Harmsworth House, currently the *West Briton*'s headquarters, on the Lemon Quay side of the "piazza".

The view ahead (compare the c.1900 photograph on page 17 of Volume 2) is dominated by the main buildings of Truro School, on the low hill beyond the river. Some information about it is given on page 74; see also Volume 2.

The redevelopment of the Lemon Quay / Back Quay area - a 3-hectare block bordered on the south by Fairmantle Street and on the west by Tabernacle Street - took place during 2000-2, following many years of controversy involving several rival plans, some of which involved opening up this part of the River Kenwyn. The pattern of streets on the south side of the river here was created at the start of the 19th century; before then the area was mainly meadows and moorland, with boatyards, rope making and other such industries

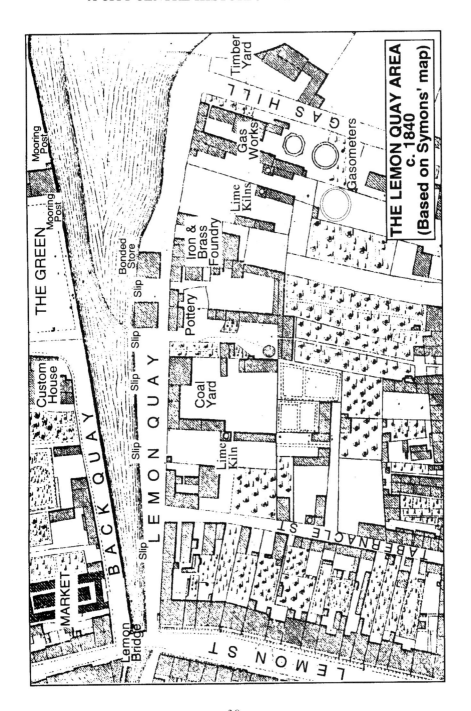

THE LEMON QUAY AREA
c. 1840
(Based on Symons' map)

beside the river. Robert Symons' mapping shows that by the 1840s this was one of Truro's main industrial centres: the gas works, especially, dominated the scene, and continued to do so right up to the 1960s. A survey carried out by the Cornwall Archaeological Unit in November and December 2000 revealed remains of a cobbler's workshop, the pottery shown on the page 39 map, and one of the lime kilns. As mentioned earlier, the process of covering over the river to provide car parking began in the 1920s and was completed during the '30s.

Immediately after passing the large shop called Quay Foodmarket, turn left into what is now known as Tinners Yard - although if the wire-mesh gates are closed you may have to content yourself with peering through them. Now used as an open-air market, it was once the site of gardens which ran down to the river - hence the name, Back Quay - and belonged to houses on Princes Street, notably the Mansion House, whose rear elevation overlooks the yard. (The front will be seen later on our walk.)

Now return to Back Quay, either by the same route or via the indoor Pannier Market, and continue to the end of the street. The large concrete-fronted market building, continuing round the corner (this part known in recent years as the Creation Centre, but now labelled "Luke's"), dates from 1934, when it was built by Hosken, Trevithick & Polkinhorn, diversifying from their corn-milling and seed-merchants' business (see page 50) into motor car sales and service, as HTP Motors Ltd. During World War 2 it was requisitioned by the government and used for the manufacture and repair of military equipment, particularly aircraft parts. The corner site was previously occupied by Truro's last Custom House; it faced on to Green Street. It was closed in 1882, when Truro was officially demoted from the status of Port to that of Creek.

Photograph by John James

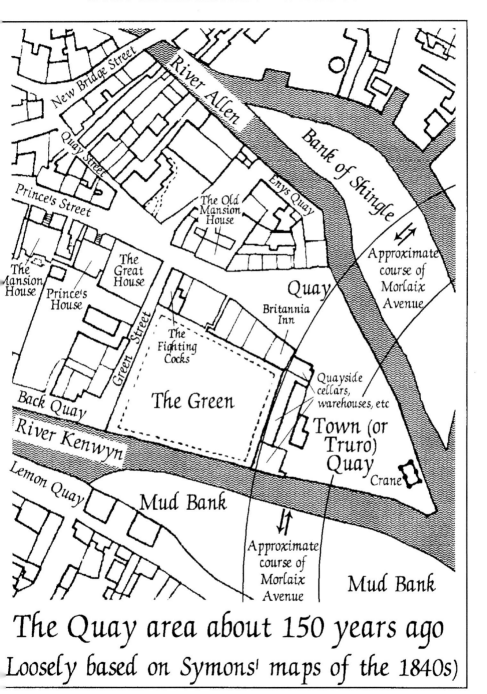

The Quay area about 150 years ago
Loosely based on Symons' maps of the 1840s)

The bus station opposite was till recently a coach and car park; much longer ago it was a bowling green (hence the name, Green Street); earlier still, it was the site of a cockpit (one of at least two in Truro: the other was in the Leats area and later became a chapel!). Despite its susceptibility to flooding at high tides, the Green was a favourite play area for children, as well as a site for fairs, parliamentary hustings and exhibitions; on one occasion it was the chosen venue for a duel at dawn involving the famous satirist, Dr John Wolcot, alias Peter Pindar (1739-1819) (▶ Vol.1,112-4). (In the event, he and his prospective assailant were reconciled in the nick of time and ate breakfast together. More details are in the Truro Buildings Group's *Princes Street and the Quay Area.*)

This is what the Lemon Quay side of the "piazza" looked like before the coming of Marks & Spencer. Included are Hicks Motors' garage and the old bus station, with the surviving Harmsworth House in the distance.
(Photograph by John James)

7 Turn left along Green Street - but first you might care to cross and go a few yards to the right for a close look at the former River Dart paddle steamer, the *Compton Castle*, now permanently based here as a florist's shop and bistro-cum-coffee-bar. It was brought to this site in 1982. Puzzle: How did they get it under the bridge? For the answer, and more about its history, see Volume 2 and the "Tourist Information" board on the other side, near the entrance to the subway.

At the far end of Green Street, notice the corner building on the right (currently "Bishop Phillpotts Fine Clothing"; in recent years it housed the SPCK shop). Beneath the rather beautiful oriel window overlooking the bus station is a crest featuring a cross, several daggers and crossed keys, and an inscription naming Henry Phillpotts, Bishop of Exeter, who presented his library (mainly theological books) to the clergy of Cornwall in 1856 - when, of course, Truro fell within his diocese. In 1869 this building was provided for the collection, which remained there until the 1980s. It is now housed in Diocesan House, part of the former premises of the Cathedral School at Kenwyn. (See Country Walk 1, page 61.)

On the Green Street wall of the same building is a plaque commemorating Richard Lander. He and his brother were born in the Fighting Cocks Inn, which stood nearby. The inn, later renamed the Dolphin Hotel and eventually the Dolphin Buttery, was eventually pulled down to enable Green Street to be widened. (Dolphins may have been particularly relevant to the Lander family, but "The Dolphin" was a common name for public houses: Leslie Douch in *Old Cornish Inns* mentions 19 in Cornwall.)

You are now entering the part of Truro most favoured by its wealthiest men in the 17th and 18th centuries for their town houses. (More detailed information about the history of this district is given towards the end of Country Walk 3, pages 94-5.) On the left, opposite the Lander plaque and continuing round the corner into Princes (or Prince's) Street, the large building occupied by the Royal Bank of Scotland is, at least in part, a restoration of the "Great House" built by the Gregor family in the second half of the 17th century. For a time it, or part of it, was the town house of the Cornish historian, the Rev. Richard Polwhele (1760-1838). One of its later 19th-century occupants was the Bodmin-born poet, Henry Sewell Stokes, who was a friend of Tennyson, and it is said that "In Memoriam" was written while Tennyson was staying there. Known to Truronians as "Blackford's" because for many years it was occupied by the printers of that name, it was badly damaged by fire in 1923. It was extensively repaired and partially rebuilt during the 1980s, but the Princes Street frontage retains much of its original character. Part of the modern building is named Penhaligon House as a tribute to our much-missed former MP, David Penhaligon.

Turn left into Princes Street.

Opposite the Princes Street entrance to the Royal Bank of Scotland stands one of the most flamboyant of Truro's smaller buildings, with its big semicircular windows and decorative patterns of brick and tile. Now "The

Old Ale House", it began as the West End Stores, specialising - as one window still announces - in "Millinery, Dressmaking, Ladies' Outfitting." More recently it belonged to Cornwall Farmers Limited.

Photograph by John James

Next to "Blackfords" and standing a few feet back from the road is perhaps the finest of all Truro's historic houses, Prince's House, built about 1740 for William Lemon (▶ Vol.1,102-4). Notice the original sash windows, with thick glazing bars. The interior is among the best in Cornwall of its period.

As late as 1881, when the 1st Edition OS map was issued, it had a large garden at the rear, twice the width of the house and extending to Back Quay. The elaborate and impressive porch and steps were added in 1893 and were designed by Silvanus Trevail.

Opposite Prince's House is another building of similar age - perhaps a few years earlier in date - which, though less imposing, is another attractive example of 18th-century town architecture. It too was built for William Lemon. Notice the Victorian pillar box beside it. It is said to be the oldest working pillar box in Cornwall: its hexagonal design dates it as pre-1879.

Next-but-one to Prince's House is the Mansion House, which again has a very fine interior. It was designed by the same architect, Thomas Edwards, some 20 years later, and the comparatively plain style of the exterior presumably reflects changing tastes. It was built for Thomas Daniell, once William Lemon's chief clerk (▶ Vol.1,108-10). On the latter's death he bought up most if not all the Lemon mining interests. He married the niece of Ralph Allen, a Cornishman who owned quarries around Bath, and the Bath stone used for the Mansion House frontage was a wedding present.

The two ancient-looking buildings almost opposite, in the Tudor or Tudor-Gothic style, in fact date only from about 1850. Between 1351 and 1848 the site of the building at the end of the street was occupied by the Coinage Hall, where ingots of tin were brought for testing and stamping before they could legally be sold (page 94 and Vol.1,28-30). The Victorian building was in recent years the Trustee Savings Bank; it currently serves as a pizza parlour, with a Victorian-style tearoom on the upper floor from which a fine panorama of Boscawen Street can be seen.

Continue ahead, re-entering Boscawen Street. Notice the plaque on this side of the successor to the Coinage Hall, mentioning that John Wesley often preached at this spot (▶ Vol.1,149). Close by is the city's War Memorial. Woolworth's stands where Gill's the drapers used to be (▶ Vol.2,28&59-60), and before Gill's The Bull, described by Christine Parnell as "once the principal inn of the town".

Cross the street and take the narrowest of Truro's opes, aptly named Squeeze Guts Alley. (It starts on the right side of Jones' shoeshop.)
8 On reaching St Mary's Street, turn right - but don't miss the impressive view left of the Cathedral, with the oldest part, St Mary's Aisle, closest. (See page 52.)

Immediately opposite the end of Squeeze Guts Alley, notice the plaque referring to the Old Grammar School, founded here in 1549 (▶ Vol.1,134-6). (For a little more about its history, see section 12, page 56, and pages 61-2.) The existing building here, dated 1730, has three original sash windows. (Whether the fake grass in front enhances it is a matter of opinion.) **Cross the Duke Street - New Bridge Street junction** (where Vage's jeweller's shop is on your left - one of Truro's oldest surviving businesses, which celebrated its centenary in September 2002)**, continuing almost straight ahead along Quay Street.** On the left side are several early-18th-century houses, mostly now converted into shops, restaurants or bars. Of particular interest are Nos. 3 & 4, currently united as "Kazbah", which date from about 1730 and still have many original details inside despite drastic alterations in recent years. The old doorway on the left outside used to give access to an open passageway.

One of the oldest of Truro's town houses (built before 1713), the Old Mansion House, is on the left as you reach the junction with Green Street - now the offices of the solicitors Hancock-Caffin. This was the home of Samuel Enys (▶ Vol.1,95-8), another man who made his fortune out of investment in mining - though he started with the advantage

of large bequests from both his grandfathers, Samuel Enys senior and Henry Gregor. (See the remarks on page 43 about "Blackford's", the "Great House", which is almost opposite.) What was probably the oldest quay on the Allen river, Enys Quay, lay behind the Old Mansion House.

Information has already been given (also on page 43) about Bishop Phillpotts' Library, the first building on the right now. It forms part of the imposing "Tudor Gothic" Victorian Public Rooms block (built late in the 1860s), mentioned on page 11 as the successor to the Assembly Rooms in High Cross. Among the many rooms, which included the Grand Lodge for the Freemasons of Cornwall, public libraries, reading rooms and facilities for billiards and chess, was a concert hall featuring a high-quality organ. The concert hall ("the largest room in the county", as reported by the contemporary local press) later became a cinema, the Palace, whose name is commemorated above one of the entrances on Quay Street.

Tacked rather incongruously to the far end of the Public Rooms, and dwarfed by them, is the Britannia Inn. Built or rebuilt in the early 1760s, it was a substantial private house, becoming an inn in 1853. Its rather isolated position beside the bypass road is very different from the days when it was one of a row of houses overlooking on one side the Green and on the other the main quay of a busy port.

On the opposite side of Quay Street, Haven House, originally the headquarters of the Haven Leisure holiday company, stands on the site once occupied by another of Silvanus Trevail's buildings, seen in a photograph on page 195 of Volume 1. Close by are sluice gates designed to control the flow of the River Allen; to judge by the rust it's some time since they were used. Damming the river at high tide and suddenly releasing the pent-up water at low tide would help to scour away some of the silt which constantly threatened, and still threatens, to make the quays unusable; in theory, too, any sewage or rubbish in the river would be carried well downstream. There was a similar arrangement on the River Kenwyn where it was crossed by Lemon Bridge - not a place where people would have lingered to admire the view!

9 **Turn left along the bypass road,** named Morlaix Avenue in honour of Truro's twin town in Brittany, **and use the subway to cross to Worth's Quay,** from which River Fal pleasure cruises can be taken when the tide is right. It is in fact the eastern end of Furniss island, which is said by some historians to have been created by centuries of garbage; Symons' map of 1848 (on page 41), however, labels it "Bank of Shingle". If you go up to the pavement beside the road and walk on to the bridge to the left (that is, towards Penrose's "Camping and Leisure" shop on Town Quay), you get quite a good view of the upper section of the Truro River. Among the modern developments on the left side of the river, such as the recently-refurbished BBC Radio Cornwall headquarters, still lurk a few dilapidated relics of the days when this part of Truro was a busy port: the (now defunct) Cathedral Glass works, for example, occupied an old building, near which used to stand two tall chimneys. Now (early 2003) only one remains. The one which has gone (the round one, shown in John James's photo) dated from 1876 and served a steam sawmill; I have yet to find out the history of the lone survivor.

The tall, distinctive "HTP" (Hosken, Trevithick & Polkinhorn) flour mill (1911) has recently been converted into residential accommodation.

Above: The HTP mill building and its neighbours, in a sorry state shortly before redevelopment
Below: a general view of this area as it was. The dredger "Reclaim" used to do a valiant job in trying to combat the huge build-up of silt.
(Both photographs by John James)

Blewett's Bakery still has its factory here, but Cornwall Farmers, part of whose Malpas Road premises was occupied by the "Wycliffe" Production Studio when that TV series was being made, has now moved to Threemilestone. The site here is due to be the new home for Cornwall and Devon Media, publishers of the *West Briton* newspaper: Harmsworth House, at Lemon Quay, is said to be "too cramped to meet modern requirements".

If you go down on to Town Quay and walk round to the left beside the railings on the quayside, you will see a line on the bridge marking the level reached by the tide on February 2nd 1885 - some three feet above the level of the quay. Also on Town Quay, beyond Penrose's, is the Truro Harbour Office.

Return through the subway, and on emerging at the far side turn left to follow the path known as River Walk, heading towards the Cathedral. At this point it runs through the gardens on Furniss Island, named after a manufacturer of sweets and biscuits (▶ Vol.2,61 etc) whose factory used to stand on the ground the other side of the water on the right, now occupied by new apartment blocks.

Furniss's factory beside the River Allen

The far bank on your left is the site of the early Enys Quay, mentioned earlier. As you approach the far end of this section of path you have one of the most-photographed (and painted) views of the Cathedral, with the "New Bridge" over the River Allen in the foreground. It was new late in the 18th century. Built at a point where there had been a ford, it provided convenient access to the town centre for traffic approaching via Mitchell Hill. (See the comments on Mitchell Hill on the opposite page.)

At New Bridge Street turn left over the bridge (not new now: it was built in 1775) **and then immediately right to continue along River Walk. Now turn left, either through the small shopping precinct called St Mary's Mews or by using the ope beyond the footbridge at the far end. Turn right on St Mary's Street.** You now have a good view (shown on page 46) of the oldest part of the Cathedral, the South Aisle added to St Mary's Church in the 16th century. Known now as St Mary's Aisle, it was much restored if not completely rebuilt during the 1880s, when, as mentioned earlier, Pearson ingeniously integrated it with the new structure. It still acts as the parish church, and the Dean of the Cathedral doubles as the Rector of St Mary's. It retains its barrel roof inside, typical of many Cornish parish churches, and is complete with its own small spire, clad with copper as a mark of the historic importance of that metal in Cornwall. The tower contains the clock mechanism which was originally installed in St Mary's church tower in 1851, and which still operates the chimes each quarter of an hour. A clock face used to project from the new tower, but that was removed for safety reasons.

Take the first right turning, Old Bridge Street. Pause to look at No.1, on the left, a fine late-18th-century building with red-brick front. Next door, just before the Barley Sheaf pub, is the little building that began in 1836 as St Mary's Sunday School. (See the photograph on page 4.) Soon you will see on your left the continuation of the River Walk, here called Wilkes Walk, in honour of Geoffrey Wilkes, Truro's Town Clerk from 1974 to 1980, when he was killed in a car crash at the age of 34. If you want to take a short cut, avoiding a rather hilly section, you could go that way, curving left past the Chapter House and Cathedral Shop. For the full walk, continue along Old Bridge Street. Old Bridge dates from at least the 13th century. It was known as East Bridge in the days when the River Kenwyn was crossed by West Bridge at what is now Victoria Square.

At the end of Old Bridge Street, cross the busy St Clement Street: recently erected traffic lights on the left side at the junction should enable you to do so in safety.

10 Take the footpath named **Rosewin Hill, almost opposite Old Bridge Street - quite steep at first, with a hand-rail.** The path curves as it ascends, passing the ends of three narrow Rosewin Rows, named Lower, Middle and East, and finally brings you to Rosewin Row itself. **Here turn left** - but first it's worth going a few yards to the right to take in the fine view of the Cathedral and surrounding buildings.

(If you were to continue in that direction to the end of Rosewin Row you would come to Mitchell Hill. This used to be the main road northwards out of Truro, and its name is an interesting reminder of the former importance of the village of Mitchell, now virtually consigned to oblivion as a result of being bypassed by the A30. Until 1832 it returned two Members of Parliament! The steepness of Mitchell Hill made it impractical for horse-drawn coaches, and Tregolls Road eventually became the main highway.)

Turning left along Rosewin Row soon brings you to Campfield Hill. Cross that, continuing almost straight ahead along Paul's Terrace. Ahead now is the Moresk Viaduct, built in 1901-4 to replace Brunel's original structure, dating from 1859. 1,329 feet long, it was the longest in Cornwall, having 20 masonry piers to support the timber superstructure. 14 of the old piers still stand. The long version of Country Walk 1 passes beneath this viaduct: see page 71.

On the right just before Paul's Terrace starts to descend is the Religious Society of Friends' (Quaker) Meeting House, an attractive and interesting building which is very fully described in the Truro Buildings Group's *From Moresk Road to Malpas*. The famous prison reformer, Elizabeth Fry, was present at the ceremony marking its opening in 1825. The Meeting House is

usually open to visitors except during services. The name on it, Truro Vean ("Little Truro"), refers to a former manor, the property of the Lanherne branch of the Arundell family.

Part of Paul's Row

Continue along Paul's Row, which now curves left downhill, and turn left at the bottom (Moresk Road) - but first you might care to cross the road and go a few yards up to the right, almost as far as the sign to Treseders Gardens. From here you get quite a good view of the slate-hung frontage of one of Truro's prettiest (if somewhat over-restored) houses, Benson House, up on the right. Built in about 1780, it was originally named Truro Vean. (The man who had it built, Peter Tippet, also set up a carpet factory nearby, which was active until 1840.)

Near the path leading to Daubuz' Moors is a notice board produced by the Cornwall Wildlife Trust describing some of the flora and fauna found there. (Daubuz' Moors is on the route of Country Walk No.1, where some information is given about this area of former watermeadows: see page 71.) For a brief comment on the Daubuz family and Treseders (pronounced, surprisingly, with the stress at the start), see the remarks about the Carvedras smelting works on page 21.

11 Go down to the foot of Moresk Road. (The Manor of Moresk, listed in the Domesday Book, became part of the estates of the Duchy of Cornwall. The site of "Moresk Castle" is on or close to the route of Country Walk 2.) The ancient Truro Vean Mills (mentioned in a document of 1337) stood on the right side of the road roughly opposite the point where Paul's Row joins it. They included fulling and corn mills, and were powered by means of a leat taken from the Allen river a good way up the Idless valley. Symons' map of 1848 shows the mill, naming it "Moresk Mill". As you cross the bridge over the Allen (1881), pause to look at the surprisingly rural scene, especially to the right (page 6). **Cross the busy St Clement Street with the aid of the central island, turning left to pass the entrance to the High Cross multi-storey car park.** Soon you will see the rear of St Mary Clement church (Truro Methodist Church) on your right. **Continue past Union Place**, noticing as you do so the particularly lovely rows of early-19th-century houses there.

12 Immediately after crossing the river again, turn right to join Wilkes Walk. On your right at first, several seats have been provided at a slightly lower level where there was once a millpool. It served Manor Mill, an undershot grist mill belonging to the manor of Truro and Treyew. The bungalows behind the seat were built as homes for the elderly in 1951 as part of Truro's contribution to the Festival of Britain - hence their name. As you cross yet another bridge over the River Allen, notice the little gents' toilet on the left - long out of use for obvious reasons of public health, but carefully preserved as a reminder of times past. In June 1999, "Tardis House", as it

"Tardis House" as it was

had been named, having been supplied with electricity and phone line, was advertised to let as an office at £25 per week. (You will have noticed that the Kenwyn also has toilets built astraddle, where it runs beneath Lemon Street; and at Victoria Square there used to be a gents' urinal, known affectionately as "The Iron Duke" or "Victoria Palace." By a strange coincidence, the Kenwyn flowed beneath that, too ...)

"Tardis House" as it now is (bottom right) and the modern Chapter House.

Fork right, passing close to the Chapter House (1967) on your left and a venerable-looking building on your right, now acting as Social Services offices. A foundation stone reveals that in fact it dates only as far back as 1908, when it became the home of the Cathedral School. It was designed by Frank Pearson, the son of the Cathedral's architect. A plan to connect it to the Cathedral by means of a cloister got no further than the one bay adjoining the Cathedral and the incomplete arches projecting from the school building, but in September 2002 the formation of a Truro Cathedral Development Project Group was announced in the local press. Its aim is to raise £6 million to complete the cloister, incorporating space to exhibit the Cathedral's treasures, currently housed in the crypt.

The other old building on the right began as a Methodist Day School, and is now Truro Young Women's Centre, opened by Princess Alexandra in 1996.

Continue beside the Cathedral shop (1987) to return to your start-point at the west end of the Cathedral.

COUNTRY WALK 1 (NORTH)
IDLESS AND IDLESS WOOD

About 9 miles from the Cathedral and back, or you could drive to Idless Wood and do a walk of just under 4 miles. Another option would be the round walk from Truro to Idless and back, omitting the woods.

The complete long walk includes Kenwyn Church, an attractive old building in a delightful setting, then about 2 miles along a quiet road on the west side of the River Allen valley. Beyond the pretty village of Idless, where there are two former watermills converted into residences, is woodland belonging to the Forestry Commission. Here you must expect to encounter timber piles, scattered branches and deeply rutted mud; wellingtons or stout walking boots will probably be needed. In the wood are a well-preserved ancient earthwork and some interesting remains of a World War 2 rifle range and a 19th century gunpowder factory. Keith Spurgin's *Wildlife Walkabouts: The Lizard to Mid-Cornwall* (probably out of print now, but should be obtainable through libraries) includes a section on the flora and fauna of Bishop's Wood. North of the wood a possible extension to the walk would take you to another former watermill. The return to Truro is via another quiet road, this time on the east side of the valley, and finally an area of watermeadow, Daubuz's Moor.

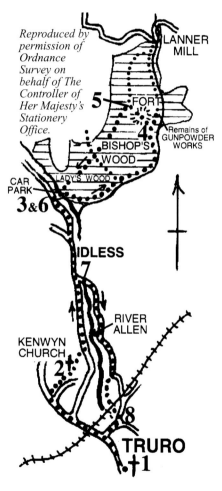

Reproduced by permission of Ordnance Survey on behalf of The Controller of Her Majesty's Stationery Office.

© **Crown Copyright**

Note: Although there are a couple of public footpaths in the woods, the walk described uses permissive paths made available to the public by the Forestry Commission. They are used by forestry vehicles, and may at times be closed to walkers, cyclists and horse-riders.

If you prefer to drive to the woods, go along Kenwyn Road and turn right at Higher Trehaverne. (There is a sign "Idless 1ˇ" at that point.) Continue up the valley through Idless and turn right where you will see a Forestry Commission sign,"Idless Wood". Parking space is provided. Directions for the woodland walk begin at point 3.

Except at times of services, you could park at Kenwyn Church: there is a wide parking area at the church end of Kenwyn Church Road. For this option, pick up walk directions at point 2. It would give you the option of shortening the walk slightly at the Truro end, as explained later.

1 To walk from the west end of the Cathedral (High Cross), turn right along Pydar Street. (Details about points of interest for the first part of the walk are given in Section 1 of the City Centre Walk; but for this one, continue along Pydar Street rather than turning left at the People's Palace.) The last building on the right as you approach the end of the pedestrianised area started life as Cornwall's second Tesco store (following Penzance) in 1978, at that time the largest supermarket in the county. (See the photo on page 185 of Volume 2.) Tesco moved to Garras Wharf in 1987.

The busy road which comes in from the right next is St Clement Street. This part of it did not exist till 1970, when it became part of an "inner circuit road", complementing the A39 relief road (now called Morlaix Avenue), which was created at about the same time. Old maps show a narrow street, Goody Lane or Goodwives Lane, roughly where the new inner circuit road now runs.

Cross with care and continue ahead, past the mini roundabout, still on Pydar Street.

The Carrick District Council Offices, on the right, were built in 1975-6: see page 178-9 in Volume 2. They were quite quickly found to be too small, and had to be supplemented with huts in the parking area behind, plus other nearby buildings such as the former employment exchange, Circuit House. At the time of writing there is much discussion of a possible move to a new site (but see the starred note on page 72). Pydar House, opposite, containing the Crown Offices, was officially opened in February 1982. The photographs on pages 156 and 179 and the map on page 152 of Volume 2 give some idea of how much this part of Truro has changed since the 1960s, when it was occupied by small town houses such as those on Boscawen Row, which once stood where the big Viaduct Car Park is.

Having passed under the railway bridge, you are on Kenwyn Road.

COUNTRY WALK 1

At the far end of the City Inn's street frontage stand two stone pillars, reputed to have been taken from the market house that till 1807 stood at the foot of King Street. The old market house was originally part of Middle Row, which divided what is now Boscawen Street into two narrow streets.

St Mary's Chapel (Mission Church), a little further up on the same side, dates from about 1850. It stands at the entrance to St Mary's Churchyard: clearly there was very little room for burials at High Cross even before the Cathedral replaced St Mary's Church. The Chapel was boarded up when I last looked at it, but notices on the door referred to possible conversion into two dwellings. In 2001 the empty building was damaged by fire, and investigators found that it was "a haven for drug users".

Among the many attractive, large houses to be seen as you continue uphill, notice particularly one of the oldest (late 18th century), the slate-hung Trehaverne House, on the right. The name is thought to derive from "Tregavran", a Domesday manor which, according to the historian Charles Henderson, was identical with the Manor of Kenwyn.

When you reach Chainwalk Drive, cross that and take the clearly signed footpath to Kenwyn Church. The path soon reveals itself to be the "chainwalk" which gives the road its name, though the chain and the sturdy granite posts are nowadays serving no obvious purpose. Old photographs show the land on the right as open fields.

KENWYN CHURCH

The name of the parish has been explained as meaning "white ridge", but Charles Henderson believed the church was dedicated to the 6th-century St Keyne, and the "brief history" which used to be available in the church confidently states that "she and her women" "settled by the ancient well which can be seen down the steps near the church porch". Alan Dunstan's guide book, the one on sale now, which includes the sister church of St Allen, makes no such claims.

There was certainly a church here by 1259, when it was dedicated by the Bishop of Exeter, Walter Bronescombe, whose name will crop up again in connection with the woodland part of this walk. Nothing as old as that appears to have survived, with the possible exception of a carved head in the south wall near the tower, but the tower and south aisle date from the 15th century.

According to the local historian Richard Polwhele, the church was "well-nigh a ruin" by the 18th century, and early in the 19th it was condemned as unsafe. A plan to demolish it and replace it with a brand-new church was

proposed, but instead a drastic restoration of the old building was carried out between 1819 and 1820 at a cost of over £1,000. Then in December 1860 lightning struck one of the pinnacles on the tower, sending blocks of masonry crashing through the roof, and this prompted a further reconstruction programme, this time under the direction of that doyen of Victorian church restorers, J.P.St Aubyn. Joseph Polsue, author of "Lake's Parochial History", considered the result "tasteful", but 20th century writers such as Charles Henderson and John Betjeman have been less complimentary. Further changes during the 20th century - mainly in the early 1960s - have aimed, in the words of Alan Dunstan, "to bring back what must have been a beautiful church."

The pretty, slate-hung room over the lychgate is said to date back to the 14th century, but was largely rebuilt early in the 19th and restored in 1985. It originally served as the priest's lodging, but from some time after 1570, when the first vicarage was built, till 1880 it was used as a school for 20-30 children. Little is known about the origin of the holy well, but it probably dates from the 4th or 5th century. Its water has long been used for baptisms. The elaborate, tall cross beside it is dedicated to the Cornish family, one of whom was vicar here in 1883 and later became the first Suffragan Bishop of St Germans.

2 Walk past the church's main door (or turn left on emerging from the church) and follow the path that runs along the edge of the churchyard. Notice at first the views over the city - best in winter, of course, when there is less foliage. (Compare the same scene as depicted in 1806, reproduced on the cover and page 4 of Volume 1.) One of the most interesting tombstones marks the grave of Joseph Emidy (d.1835), "Slave, Violinist, Composer". That is the subtitle of Dr McGrady's fascinating book about him and his contemporaries, *Music and Musicians in Early 19th-Century Cornwall* (University of Exeter Press, 1991). Dr McGrady says the grave is "deep in the shade of a fir tree". Perhaps that will help you to find it; so far my wife and I have failed!

Steps down on the right from the path lead to the modern building now named Diocesan House. It was officially opened in September 1960 as a classroom block and library for Truro Cathedral School. If you go down the steps and turn left (not a right of way, as far as I know, but you are unlikely to be challenged if you use it) you will reach the large, impressive building currently bearing the name Epiphany House, but better known as Copeland Court.

COPELAND COURT

The oldest part of it was built in the late 1770s as Kenwyn Vicarage. John Wesley stayed there, and described it as "a house fit for a nobleman". In 1877, by which time it had been much enlarged, it became Lis Escop, the Palace of the Bishop of Truro. (The parish priest then moved into a smaller vicarage beside the church: it is now called Frere House, after Bishop Walter Frere.) Bishop Benson described the older building as "more like a small country-house than a vicarage". "Small" may seem an odd adjective for a house with thirteen bedrooms, even if there was only one bathroom, but Truro's fourth Bishop, Charles William Stubbs, declared that there was hardly room for his own family, let alone visitors, so the noted architect Edmund Sedding was engaged to make further additions, including a big dining room.

The beauty of the large garden owes much to Bishop Hunkin. When he moved in, in 1935, the gardener described the grounds as "a mess"; but over the next decade Hunkin became a noted horticulturalist. Details of his contribution to Lis Escop can be found in Douglas Ellory Pett's "The Parks and Gardens of Cornwall" (1998) and especially "From a Cornish Bishop's Garden" (2002), both published by Alison Hodge.

The house fell vacant when Hunkin's successor, Bishop Morgan, moved to the former St Mary's Rectory in Kenwyn Road. In 1953 the former Lis Escop was bought by the Copeland family, owners of the Trelissick estate at Feock, and presented to the Cathedral School in memory of their son Ronald, a former pupil at the school who was killed during the Suez conflict. The school adopted it for its junior section in 1954 and re-named it Copeland Court. In the early 1960s the Copelands provided a new Bishop's Palace at Trelissick. (The Cathedral School closed in 1982; its demise led to the founding of the Duchy Grammar School at Tregye, near Carnon Downs. That in turn finally closed in July 1999.) Following the closure of the Cathedral School, Copeland Court became Epiphany House, as explained in Volume 2 (page 250). The Community of the Epiphany ceased to exist in 2001, and the house and grounds were offered to let, but at the time of writing (late 2002) it was still vacant.

Continue along the churchyard path, which, after passing a comparatively recent extension of the burial ground, bears right, then left, then right again. At this last corner, go down the stepped path ahead. (It is known as "40 Steps", an interesting example of Cornish counting.) **Turn right on to the lane at the bottom, and at the road turn left.** The walk now continues for a mile or more along this usually very quiet country road. The River Allen is down to your right all the way, mostly a little too far off to be seen or heard.

As you approach Idless, you will see the river quite close; the walk route later crosses the old stone bridge you will glimpse down below, and gives you a close look at the interesting buildings beside it; but first, walk on through the village.

IDLESS

The name, pronounced "eedless" and often spelt "Edless" till recent times, may derive from a Cornish phrase meaning "place of aspens"; if so it is in good company with several other local names alluding to trees: Gwarnick ("place of alders"), Killagorden and Killivose (in which the first element means "grove"), Penhellick (Cornish, heligen, willows) ... An alternative explanation of "Idless", however, is that it is a corruption of "Edelet", the name given in the Domesday Book to the ancient manor in which it was located; the nearby small settlement of Allet certainly gets its name from that source.

It seems there was a settlement here before Truro existed: it lies on what was once an important route between the Gannel on the north coast and the Truro River on the south. It ran through Bishop's Wood, entering the Allen Valley at Idless to reach navigable waters at Trehaverne. (See the maps on pages 15 and 17 in Volume 1.)

COUNTRY WALK 1

Idless is a sleepy little village now, but in the days when water power was fully exploited its two mills would have been busy. A mineral lode containing mainly lead and iron but also silver in places runs north-south nearby - it may be the same lode that yielded such riches for East Wheal Rose, near St Newlyn East. (See "Around St Agnes & Perranporth" and "Exploring Cornish Mines" Volume 3.) Garras Mine, situated near Gwarnick, a short way north of Idless, was active by 1700, and several blowing houses were at work in and round Idless from about that time: see the later note on Scawswater Mill. As well as water power, these would have required a supply of charcoal from the nearby woodland. Some if not all would have had batteries of stamps. Garras Mine's most productive period was during the first half of the 19th century, when it had a steam engine for pumping and a lot of other machinery, and was profitable enough to set up its own smelting works in Truro: hence the name, Garras Wharf, now the site of Tesco and its neighbouring car parks. But the mine ceased working in 1851, and although two other mines (South and East Garras) started up soon afterwards, both had closed by 1860. This was not the end of industrial activity nearby, however: see the later note about the gunpowder factory in Bishop's Wood.

Almost as soon as you have passed the "Idless" sign, Idless Mill is on your right, now an impressive private house.

IDLESS MILL

A watermill stood here by the 16th century. A "new mill" mentioned in a document of 1644 valued it at £6.13s.4d.; at the same date a bible belonging to the leaseholder was valued at 2s.6d., so the mill was apparently worth only about 53 books. Detailed records survive of a dispute about ownership which began in 1717 and was apparently still not settled by 1898!

The surviving mill buildings probably date from the early 19th century. They comprised a three-storey grist mill containing corn loft, milling loft with two pairs of stones, and mill chamber. The overshot waterwheel was equipped with "crown gear". A lean-to contained two corn or meal stores, stabling etc. A fee of a pound a year was paid for allowing the water to flow unimpeded through the mill leat, which was taken from the River Allen at a point close to the main entrance to Idless Wood. The Hawkey family were millers here for many years. Idless Mill was sold by the Tregothnan Estate in 1919 (reserve price, £1,000), and it appears to have ceased production soon after that.

COUNTRY WALK 1

، *Idless Mill*
The Truro Buildings Research Group's publication, "Idless and the River Allen" (1993) gives plenty of fascinating information about this mill's history.

Continue along the road through the village. Soon you pass an attractive group of cottages on the left - actually converted barns; later come the former United Methodist Chapel (on the right near the telephone kiosk) and the pretty former Church of the Good Shepherd, almost opposite. The latter was a Mission Church served by the Vicar of Kenwyn. An article of reminiscences by Mrs Eileen Arnold in *Idless and the River Allen* makes clear how important a part in village life the chapel and church once played. Both are now private houses - the church since the early 1970s and the chapel even longer.

Not far away to your right at this point is where a dam has been built with sluice gates in order to control the flow of the River Allen in the event of flood danger: see Volume 2, page 223.

Ignore the road off to the left and go on past the turning to Woodpark. The house called Woodlands, on the left here, was an ale house, the Woodman's Arms, until it closed, during or immediately after World War 1.

3 **Turn right at the Forestry Commission notice, Idless Wood.**

IDLESS WOOD

There are in fact three woods, the largest being Bishop's Wood, so named because it was once owned by the Bishopric of Exeter, which bought it as part of the Manor of Cargoll in 1269. In 1258 Bishop Walter Bronescombe had bought from King Henry III the right to create deer parks for hunting, and he had the woodland close to the Bishop's Palace at Lanner enclosed for this purpose. (The Palace itself is thought to have been where Lanner Barton now stands, on the northern side of the wood.) The first part of the walk passes through Lady's Wood, and further west is Lord's Wood; I have not come across any explanation of those names. Confusingly, the woodland as a whole was till recently called St Clement Wood, although it lies outside St Clement parish.

In the latter part of the 15th century the bishops ceased visiting their three Cornish deer parks; they were let to tenants and eventually sold. During the following centuries the sessile oaks in the three woods were coppiced for fuel, and bark was sold to tanneries such as Croggon's at Grampound. Charcoal burning, lime burning and gunpowder manufacture took place in the woods at various periods.

Idless Wood was bought by the Forestry Commission in 1951. They have carried out a programme of replanting, mainly of conifers, although the proportion of deciduous trees has increased in recent years.

Go through the gap beside the wooden gate at the far end of the parking area. You are on a wide, well-made track at first - actually a forestry road. Where that bends left, go straight on. This track, somewhat narrower, keeps close to the edge of the woodland, and before long you will see a stream down to your right. Modern maps mark this as a tributary of the River Allen, into which it flows at Idless, though the First Edition OS map (1880) names it River Allen.

Continue on the main track, passing several paths which go up into the woods on your left. The first obvious example is where two such paths start, the right-hand one being one of the public footpaths mentioned earlier, as indicated by the yellow waymark arrow on a wooden post. (This path marks the boundary between Bishop's Wood and Lady's Wood. For much of its length it runs in a ditch with a high bank on the left (Lady's Wood) side, features which probably survive from the deer park. The bank would have been topped by oak fencing in an effort to keep the agile deer in.)

Next comes an uphill track, at the start of which is a post inscribed 6Z. (You will see many more such posts as you walk on; they are for the benefit of orienteers.)

When you come to another path up to the left, still keep to the lower track, but notice the substantial building below to your right here. Built of masonry and concrete, with rusty iron pillars supporting an overhang, it is some 50 feet long, with a further length of wall at the far end. Steps (probably slippery in damp weather) lead down into it. This is what survives of the rifle range mentioned in the introduction. A gentleman my wife and I spoke to remembered using it during the last war. The butts were up in the fields to the south-east, at or near Penmount Farm: the remains of one of them can, I'm told, still be found.

4 Take the next left fork, which comes quite soon after the rifle range. But first, if you are at all interested in industrial archaeology, continue a few yards further along the level track, and you will have a good view, down to your right, of the remains of the factory set up early in the 1860s by the Cornwall Blasting Powder Company. Leats can be seen running both above and below a group of ruined stone buildings, and the remains of wheelpits have also survived. (See the photograph on the back cover.)

Those who have visited Kennall Vale, near Ponsanooth, will recognise that here too there were several pairs of incorporating mills, each pair powered by one overshot waterwheel. The following note owes much to Bryan Earl's account in *Cornish Explosives*.

COUNTRY WALK 1
GUNPOWDER MANUFACTURE IN BISHOP'S WOOD

The Cornwall Blasting Powder Company (apparently also known as the St Allen Powder Company) began work here in 1863, at a time when mining and quarrying in Cornwall were flourishing and the demand for gunpowder was high. The site was good for the purpose, being well away from any residential area but with fairly easy acces to the port of Truro; there was a ready supply of water to power machinery and of timber for the charcoal which was one of the essential ingredients. The works included a sawmill. Although the operation was quite small, with a workforce of about 14 and annual production never more than about 300 tons, it was reasonably profitable in its early years. By the mid-1870s, however, mining was in decline and gunpowder was being superseded by "high explosives" such as guncotton and nitroglycerine, and the company began making attempts to sell off the works as a going concern. No buyer could be found, and when the mills were put up to let in 1883 there was again no taker. The machinery was broken up for scrap in 1887.

Although there is so much less to see here than at Kennall Vale, the manufacturing process was basically the same, so it may be useful if I repeat here the very simplified account of it which I included in "Exploring Cornwall's Tramway Trails", Volume 2.

The raw materials (charcoal, saltpetre and sulphur) were mixed in a rotating wooden barrel in a Mixing House, and taken to an Incorporating Mill, where the mixture was dampened and ground to a fine powder by two vertically-mounted millstones. Then it went to a Press House to be compressed into a "cake" about an inch thick; next this was broken (using wooden mallets) into lumps in a Breaking House, then reduced to granules in a Corning House, dried by means of piped steam in a Gloom Stove, and separated from dust in a Dusting House. Finally the granules were rounded and glazed (so that they could easily be poured into holes and were water-resistant - important in damp mine-workings) by being rotated in a drum with graphite in a Glazing Mill, before being packed in wooden crates. "Expense Magazines" were used for storage between processes.

Several accidents at the Bishop's Wood factory were reported in the press, some of them resulting in deaths. Bryan Earl gives details, as does "Idless and the River Allen". One incident, in 1868, is said to have involved explosions so violent that they were "mistaken for an earthquake in Truro, two miles away". 20 cwt of powder had gone up, but no one was killed on that occasion.

COUNTRY WALK 1

The uphill track soon brings you to a Forest Enterprise notice and a smaller one announcing that you are about to reach the moat and earth wall of the ancient fort. It is described by Craig Weatherhill as "Iron Age/ Romano-British", which would indicate that it dates back about two thousand years. Although not on the very highest ground, it presumably commanded wide views before the trees took over. **The path continues across the centre of the earthwork and out through a similar gap to the one you entered by.**

5 When you reach the wide track (in fact the same forestry road you were on for a short distance at the start of the woodland walk), either turn left to return to the car park by the most direct route: simply keep to the forestry road all the way; or turn right for a there-and-back extension of the walk (about a mile in all) to the northern exit from the wood. For this option, continue along the forestry road for half a mile or so. About 200 yards beyond the second large clearing it bears right; at the next fork, keep left, and you are soon back by the stream. Turn left on this track, and a few yards further on is the gate by which you leave the wood. On reaching the road there it would be worth turning right and walking the few yards down past Lanner Mill - another impressive conversion - to the old bridge. Return to point 5 by the same route and continue along the forestry road to the car park.

6 From the main entrance to the woods, if you are walking back to Truro turn left and go back through Idless.

7 After Idless Mill take the left fork and cross the bridge, where another watermill used to be.

SCAWSWATER MILL

The substantial ruins of a 17th-century blowing house have survived here. They are not visible from the road, but stand in the garden behind the recently rebuilt and converted 19th century mill near the bridge. (A blowing house was an early form of tin-smelting house, fuelled by charcoal. The temperature in the furnace was raised by bellows driven by a waterwheel.) A tucking (fulling) mill with spinning jenny was working at Scawswater by 1824, probably using the former blowing-house building. Early maps indicate quite a large group of buildings on the site. The poster advertising them for sale in 1847 as "a large and commodious Manufactory, heretofore used as a Woollen and Serge Manufactory" is reproduced in H.L.Douch's "The Book of Truro". After that the tall mill building next to the cottage was in use as a sawmill;

and finally it worked as a grist mill until ceasing operations in the 1920s. A large overshot waterwheel powered the various processes. It was fed by a leat taken from the stream which runs along the eastern edge of Idless Wood, where its mill pool was. The building suffered fire damage and was in a state of severe dilapidation when the present owners decided to have it restored as far as possible to its original appearance; luckily, several photographs of it in its working days exist as a guide, such as the one reproduced on the previous page, showing it in its time as a sawmill, and another in Sheila Bird's "Bygone Truro". The work began in 1995 and is still ongoing.

The road beyond has high banks, but you get occasional glimpses of the marshy River Allen valley to your right. After nearly half a mile you will see on your left the gatehouse and impressive wrought-iron gates at the end of the long drive to Killagorden. The mansion itself, an old one rebuilt late in the 18th century, is not visible from the road, but there is a drawing of it in "Idless and the River Allen", which also includes the memories of a lady who worked there as a maid from 1927 to 1931. Down to the right nearby is Killagorden (or Killagordon) Farm.

When you come to woodland, you will probably hear if not see the weir and sluice down to the right, at the point where a leat (millrace) begins. The leat, well preserved but now no longer flowing, runs close to the road for much of its length. It was constructed to power the Moresk Mills at Truro Vean.

MORESK MILLS

Corn and fulling mills for the Duchy Manor of Moresk are mentioned in a document as early as 1337. The corn mill was rebuilt in the mid-19th century, and eventually it had two overshot waterwheels and a compound tandem condensing engine. Over the next few decades its output was over 1000 sacks of flour per week, with a turnover of about £100,000 per annum. This mill is marked on Robert Symons' 1848 Plan of the Borough of Truro: top-left corner of the section of it reproduced inside the front cover of Volume 1. The milling company, which had offices in Pydar Street, ceased trading before the end of the 19th century, but I have been told that in later years the leat supplied water to the Truro Steam Laundry, Moresk Road: see Volume 2, pages 193-4. This may be why it is still so well preserved.

After a short downhill stretch, where a sign warns that the road is liable to flooding, you will pass a cottage on the left. Soon after that, take

the footpath on the right where there is a wooden post marked "Moresk Road", along with an information board about Daubuz's Moors, provided by the Cornwall Wildlife Trust. Cross the little bridge over the millrace and bear left. Lewis Charles Daubuz (1754-1839) planted spectacular gardens on the east side of the watermeadows. (There is more about the Daubuz family and their involvement in tin smelting on pages 21-2.) The area once occupied by the gardens, now residential, bears the names "Nursery Close" and "Treseder's Gardens", references to the well-known nursery which was founded there in 1838 and closed as recently as 1982. (Say Treseder, stressing the first syllable, but using the short "e", as in "tremble".) The "Moors" were given to the citizens of Truro in 1977 by the Enys family to mark the Queen's Silver Jubilee.

Beside the arches of the modern viaduct are the piers which once supported the wooden superstructure carrying Brunel's broad-gauge railway line. His Moresk Viaduct (1858) was, at just over 1,300 feet, the longest in Cornwall, with twenty masonry piers, fourteen of which still stand. John Binding's *Brunel's Cornish Viaducts* (Pendragon, 1993) has several photos of it, including one from 1902 which shows the all-masonry replacement under construction. The first train ran over the new viaduct on 14th February 1904.

8 **At Moresk Road, <u>either</u> (a) if you parked at Kenwyn Church or Idless Wood and don't want to include the city centre in your walk, turn right, crossing the River Allen by the road bridge** (1881; look right for the surprisingly rural view shown on page 6), **then right again at the T-junction (St Clement Street).** Continue past Circuit House, which opened as an Employment Exchange (Job Centre) in 1970. Its name reflects the fact that it was the first new building on this road, constructed as part of the "inner circuit" during the late 1960s. **At the mini roundabout, go on up Pydar Street, with the Carrick District Council offices* on your right, and pick up the directions in section 1.**

* (If they are still there when you do this walk: controversial plans to replace them with "a large department store and 35 shops", thus "increasing the city's retail space by a third" during the next four years, were announced in the local press during April 2003.)

Or (b), to continue to the Cathedral, cross Moresk Road with care and take the road almost opposite the end of the path, Paul's Terrace.

Over to the left is the attractive late-18th-century mansion, originally called Truro Vean House but now named Benson House in honour of Truro's first Bishop. Its first owner was Peter Tippet, who set up close by a carpet factory, which continued working till 1840. A visitor to it in 1795 reported that about 700 men, women and children were employed there or at the spinning jenny and dye works near the Mill Pool which this walk route passes soon.

On the left at the start of Paul's Terrace, behind a high wall, is Truro's Quaker Meeting House, built in the garden of Truro Vean House in 1825, when the house was owned by members of the Society of Friends. (There is more about it on pages 53-4.) The Meeting House is usually open to visitors except during services.

At the T-junction turn right, down Campfield Hill; cross the busy St Clement Street (there is a pedestrian crossing with traffic lights), and take Wilkes Walk, almost opposite Campfield Hill, passing the Mill Pool, and turning right to return to High Cross at the west end of the Cathedral.

COUNTRY WALK 2 (EAST)
ST CLEMENT, TRESILLIAN & MALPAS

About seven and a half miles. If you omit Tresillian, about five miles - and the walk can be reduced to about three miles by cutting out St Clement too.

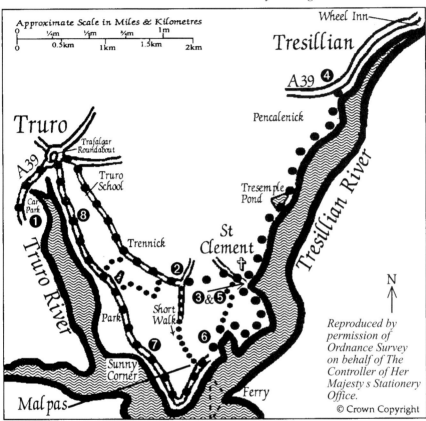

A very pretty walk, mostly beside the waters of the Truro and Tresillian Rivers. St Clement is a charming and peaceful tiny waterside village with a picturesque old church; Malpas is rather larger and busier, at least in summer, when there is much boating activity. It commands fine views over the two rivers. Tresillian is spoilt by the main road, but the walk there from St Clement is lovely, affording good views of the quiet shores of the Tregothnan estate opposite. There is a mile or more of road walking in Malpas and from there to Truro, but all of it is attractive and not normally busy; most of the way there is a pavement or roadside path. Currently, three buses a day run between Truro and Malpas, Monday to Saturday: Truronian Service 6. There is a very popular pub, the Heron, at Malpas, where you can also find a small shop; the well-known Wheel Inn at Tresillian is unfortunately too far along the A39 to be of much use to you on this walk. There are public toilets in St Clement and Malpas.

The first part of the route is from Truro to St Clement across country, along back roads and lanes and through fields, with occasional glimpses of the water. One section is usually very muddy, so please use suitable footwear. If you walk on from St Clement to Tresillian you have to return by the same path, unless, of course, you take a bus back to Truro from Tresillian ... but it would be a shame to miss Malpas.

This is an area rich in footpaths, most if not all of which seem to be well maintained and clearly signed, so if you arm yourself with the Explorer map you could quite easily work out several other attractive round walks - for example, visiting St Clement and Malpas but not Truro. In that case it would be wise to start at Malpas and use the bus to get there, because there is little room for parking in either village.

Even if you intend to keep to one of the routes I am about to recommend I suggest you take a map, just in case the permissive waterside path from St Clement to Malpas is closed - unlikely but possible, as explained later.

For much of the information that follows I am indebted to June Palmer and the other members of the Truro Buildings Research Group, who in 1988 and 1991 published their excellent studies, *From Moresk Road to Malpas* and *In and Around St Clement Churchtown.*

The directions are given from the main long-stay car park in Truro, near the big Tesco store beside the main road (Morlaix Avenue, the A39).

1 Walk to the busy Trafalgar roundabout where St Austell Street meets the A39 (Tregolls Road), take the turning signposted to St Clement (i.e. St Clement's Hill), and almost immediately turn right, up Trennick Lane. This takes you through the grounds of Truro School, an independent school founded by the Methodist Church in 1880. To quote from David Mudd's *Around the City* (Bossiney Books), "It is almost impossible to believe that Truro School, with its imposing buildings and beautiful site, was bought, built and equipped for a mere £10,000." See Volume 2 for details of the history of Truro School.

Continue up the tarmacked road for about half a mile (notice the view to the right of the Truro River, including the factories and warehouses of Newham), **until it reaches a farm (Trennick).**

This sketch is based on an old photograph of Truro River, with Garras Wharf on the right - long before Tesco arrived there.

Till the road along the shore was made (and the earliest map I can find that shows it complete dates from 1848), the only way from Truro to Malpas was along Trennick Lane to Park Farm and then south.

For a very short walk, you could take the signed path on the right here, passing the grounds of Trennick House on your left, and turning right when you reach the road at the bottom.

But to continue towards St Clement, take the track straight ahead, keeping left of the buildings. Before long it becomes a path, quite rough underfoot, then widens again. From here on it is a sunken lane, probably an old packhorse road. At the valley bottom it is crossed by a stream. There's a footbridge here now, but in wet periods things can still be pretty sticky around it. **The track continues up the other side of the valley** - in May it is heavy with the scent (if that's the word) of onion from the "white bluebells" which line it.

A second signed path on the right offers another chance of shortening the walk considerably: this one would take you past the Georgian house

known as Park and bring you down to the riverside road beside the small lake close to the Mill House (now Trennick Mill restaurant). Little seems to be known about the corn mill that used to stand nearby, apart from the fact that it had been converted from water to steam power by 1820.

But for the full route still press on ahead.

2 When you reach the road,

Either: TO OMIT ST CLEMENT turn right. The road soon becomes a bridleway, increasingly muddy as it continues. At the point where there are three field entrances, keep on in the same direction, passing through one of the farm gates to join a grassy path. This takes you direct to Malpas, with a steep descent into the village. (As mentioned earlier, until early in the 19th century this was the only way to and from Malpas and the ferry!) There are excellent views at several points on this section of the walk, perhaps best of all if you look to the left soon after joining the grassy path. From here you can see two short sections of the Tresillian River, with Pencalenick house in the middle distance, Tresillian village beyond, and the tall tower of Probus church further right. On the skyline are the huge waste tips of china-clay country, around St Austell. Much further right, the squat little spire of St Michael Penkevil church peeps above the trees on a hilltop. Walk with care down the long flight of steps: it's all too easy to be distracted by the water view below. You eventually emerge at the road opposite the ferry point; turn right for the pub and Truro, following the directions from point 6 line 8.

Or: TO INCLUDE ST CLEMENT, turn left on the road and then immediately right. After the metal 5-bar gate, continue straight ahead, with the hedge on your left at first, and then across the field. Should you have difficulty following the path, keep more-or-less to the line of the telegraph wires and you should find the wooden gate that brings you back on to the clear, sunken path. Turn left when you reach a T-junction with a track leading to a house on the right. After passing the St Clement Parish Hall, turn right down the hill into St Clement. Notice the well and pump on the right after a few yards.

There are public toilets further down, also on the right.

Take the left turning to the church - but just before doing so, notice the unusual collection of cups and mugs which decorates an old stone shed, roughly opposite the turning.

The church has a slate-hung room over its lych gate. Liz Luck says this "has served as parish vestry room, village school, Sunday school and pigsty."

The church itself, with its attendant cottages - straw birds perched on top of the small thatched roofs of the porches of one - tempts every photographer who sees it. The middle cottage on the left was the Ship Inn from at least 1844 till its closure in about 1908.

Continue ahead through the lych gate and the churchyard, eventually leaving that via a gate on the far side; turn right then left to walk down to the riverside.

ST CLEMENT

The parish's patron saint was a first-century pope who is said to have been martyred by being tied to an anchor and thrown into the sea: this may be why he has been adopted by Trinity House, which is responsible for Britain's lighthouses. Whether you call the parish and village "St Clement" or "St Clements" seems to be a matter of taste; its ancient name was quite different - Moresk. (See the later note on Denas Road.) J.B.A.Hockin, in his wonderfully rich and readable book, "Walking in Cornwall" (1936), calls it "a tiny unfrequented village in a setting that delights me more than St Just's because it is less posed." He then spoils the effect somewhat by adding, "The church has the most hideous stained glass I have ever seen." (Is this really the same church John Betjeman described in his Shell Guide? "... with pretty patterned glass inside the windows, red, blue and yellow on a clear ground, which give

77

a twinkling Victorian effect".) The church dates from the 14th century (the date 1326 is cut into the tower) but was largely rebuilt in 1865. A point of interest inside is the Polwhele Aisle, dedicated to the important local family of that name. The door to it may be locked, but you will still be able to read the wall plaque which commemorates Richard Polwhele (1760-1838), who while Vicar of Manaccan near Helford wrote a famous history of Cornwall.

Hockin goes on to refer to the well-known inscribed stone (then standing in the vicarage garden, but now near the porch), which "apparently did duty over two separate post-Roman graves before being adapted into a Celtic, wheel-headed cross." Known as the Ignioc Stone, it is dedicated to a Roman, Vitalis, son of Torricus, who probably lived early in the 6th century AD; the word "Ignioc" appears to have been added in about 600. At Yealhampton in Devon is a similar stone thought by some to be dedicated to Ignioc's father. The stone at St Clement is commonly said also to have inscriptions in Ogham, a Celtic alphabet normally used only in Ireland, but Professor Charles Thomas, the former Director of Cornish Studies, has denied this claim.

The churchyard also has several interesting headstones; one, for example (also close to the porch, but on the opposite side from the Ignioc Stone) celebrates a devoted female servant who requested that her wages should be reduced because as she grew ever more elderly she became increasingly incapable of carrying out the domestic chores.

3 When you get down to the waterside, if you want to limit the walk to about five miles turn right and follow the directions from No. 5; if you prefer to walk on to Tresillian turn left and keep to the path which follows the edge of the river all the way there.

Looking towards Tresillian from St Clement

The large house on fairly high ground which can be seen almost straight ahead immediately after you have passed the last of the cottages at St Clement is Pencalenick. It was built on the site of a much older house in 1881 for Michael Williams of Tredrea (Perranarworthal), the architect having been J.P.St Aubyn, a name much reviled by John Betjeman for his many insensitive "restorations" of Cornish churches. (Compare page 60.) Following its requisition to accommodate military personnel during World War 2 (first British troops, then Americans, and finally Italian prisoners of war), Pencalenick was bought by Cornwall County Council and converted into a school for disabled children.

The water on your left at one point is Tresemple Pond, and all the quiet woodland on the far bank is part of the Tregothnan Estate, the seat of the Boscawen family, Lord and Lady Falmouth.

4 The path, after joining a small road for a few yards, brings you out on to the A39 at Tresillian. This hardly makes for pleasant walking, but if you turn right and continue for at least half a mile your efforts will be rewarded by The Wheel Inn.

COUNTRY WALK 2
TRESILLIAN & THE WHEEL INN

The Inn dates from the 14th century. In the Civil War it was General Fairfax's headquarters when the Cornish Royalists under Hopton finally surrendered, at Tresillian Bridge. (The bridge is further along, where the main road bends left, and the long drive to Tregothnan starts at the gatehouse on the right. Inside the church at the corner is a plaque commemorating the Parliamentary victory.) On New Year's Eve each year a hundred guests at the Wheel tuck into a huge Cornish pasty, eight stone in weight and six feet long.

If you've had enough walking now, there are plenty of buses to Truro from Tresillian (although of course they are few and far between when you're waiting for one). The intrepid walkers need to **return to St Clement by the same waterside path.**

Back at St Clement

5 **At St Clement, continue along the waterside path, here named Denas Road.** **Please note:** As mentioned in my introductory comments, this is a concessionary or permissive path, not a right of way. The landowner could close it, and did in fact threaten to do so a few years back in response to vandalism. If you need to find an alternative route to Malpas, there is a field path which starts almost opposite the church, climbs nearly to the top of the hill - the likely site of Moresk Castle - and then descends quite steeply to the small creek on the edge of Malpas.

COUNTRY WALK 2
DENAS ROAD

This footpath was created by Conservation Volunteers in 1986. Its name, found often elsewhere in forms like Dinas, Dennis and Pendennis, means "fort", and here it refers to Moresk Castle, which is believed once to have stood about half way between St Clement and Malpas, where it could guard both the landing place at the former and the ferry-point at the latter. It was apparently destroyed in the 12th century, during a civil war between King Stephen and his cousin Mathilda. St Clement was part of the ancient Manor of Moresk or Morrois (a name which may derive from the French "marais", marshy place), which extended as far north as St Erme and included part of Truro. It is an area linked in history and legend with Tristan and Isolda: after her husband, King Mark, discovered that they were lovers they fled to the Forest of Morrois. See also the note about Malpas.

The waterside path is especially attractive, with views towards Tresillian at one end and towards Malpas at the other, and is well endowed with wild flowers, particularly in spring. **There are several stiles, one of them a ladder stile which demands some care in crossing. Yellow arrows on wooden posts guide the way, but you can hardly go wrong so long as you keep close to the water. At the head of a small inlet, "Denas Road" joins the**

Looking towards Malpas

**other path, mentioned earlier as a possible alternative, and you follow it
over a plank bridge and into Malpas.**

MALPAS

*Old maps locate "Mopus" or "Mopas" on the far (St Michael Penkevil) side
of the water; the 1813 OS map gives no hint of any settlement on the north
shore here, but as the village developed during the next few decades the name
came to be applied to it.*

*Many local people say the name as spelt on the old maps, but it's often
pronounced with its first syllable to rhyme with "fall". It derives from the
French "le mal pas", bad step, i.e. difficult ford. Oliver Padel comments,
"The name is likely to have been given in the 12th century, and suggests that
the river here was regularly, though unpleasantly, crossed at that period."
Legend tells that, disguised as a leper, Tristan, nephew of King Mark of
Cornwall, carried Iseult (Isolda) across the river at Malpas. It's hard to
believe it could be done, even with the help of planks laid across the mud,
because the water was presumably deeper in the 6th century, silting-up having
occurred later. Perhaps one should interpret the tale as evidence of how
ancient the triangular ferry service here is. A name frequently mentioned in
connection with it is that of "Jenny Mopus" (actual name Jane Davis), a
muscular lady who achieved great feats early last century as an oarswoman
and is often quoted as declaring that the hardest part of her job was dealing
with "Wemmin & Pigs."*

*Quite large cargo vessels still pass Malpas occasionally on their way to
dock at Newham, Truro, and until recently there was a fuel depot at Malpas,
now replaced by bijou residences. The wife of the ferryman, whose pretty
cottage is on the headland on the Tregothnan side, told me of her regret at the
change: when the ships used to moor there the crews made friends with the
family at the cottage, and sometimes at night they were asked to leave their
lights on to guide the ships round the bend. She also said that formerly there
was a big heronry nearby among the Woodbury trees, but the noise caused by
the building work drove the herons down-river. (Another explanation given
for their departure is that the colony was practically wiped out by the severe
winter of 1962-3 - ironically, at about the same time as the one surviving pub
in Malpas changed its name from the Park Inn to the Heron. Park, as mentioned
earlier, is the attractive Georgian house north of Malpas, close to the walk
route.)*

Despite such perhaps regrettable changes, it's obviously not just the excellent food at the Heron that makes so many people flock to Malpas. I can't resist ending, as the Truro Buildings Research Group did, with the description of Malpas printed in the Royal Cornwall Gazette of January 1870: "The serpentine course of its waters, the thickly wooden (sic) banks, quick succession of hill and dale, and the ever varying shades of colour give a peculiar liveliness to this favourite resort of Truronians." It's still true.

6 From here on, it's simply a matter of following the road through the village. Just before you reach the steep path down into the village mentioned earlier, opposite the quay used by the ferry, you will pass the house called Riverview, the home of Philip Plumbley, a former sea captain whose retirement hobby is carving and painting wooden figureheads. Some of them are usually displayed above his garage, one door of which is labelled "Master" and furnished with a porthole.

Continue past the Heron (opposite which the buses to Truro depart), and on for a further two miles into Truro. The public toilets down on the left became quite famous for a while in 2002 because they were adopted by a chicken which then stoutly defended its new territory against all intruders! **Soon after leaving the village, you can avoid walking beside the road by taking the path down by the water's edge.**

Looking down the Truro River at Sunny Corner

7 **At Sunny Corner you have to return to the road for a short stretch, but just beyond the Truro Cricket Club ground you can walk through the playing fields and park,** which were developed during the late 1880s on what had been timber pounds and mud flats. (This is Boscawen Park, named from Lord Falmouth, who provided much of the land for it. A covered performing area was being constructed in May 2002 when I last walked here, and a dead tree beside it was being transformed into a tall sculpture.) When the railway came to Truro during the 1850s, one proposal was for the line to cross the river a little way north (that is, on the Truro side) of where the park now is to reach the terminus at Newham; nowadays the threat is from the internal combustion engine, since many people argue that Truro desperately requires a southern bypass road, and that it should cross the Truro River hereabouts.

8 As you enter Truro you will see commercial wharves on the far bank, as well as the relics of several now defunct factories and warehouses on this side, notably the HTP building, now converted into waterside apartments. (In fact, by 2003 nearly all the old factories and warehouses on Malpas Road had been demolished or converted into residential accommodation or offices.) This walk shows quite well what isn't always noticed by visitors: that Truro was once an important port, and still has ambitions in that direction. See Volumes 1 and 2 and Country Walk 3.

You can escape some of the ugliness of the last few hundred yards of the road, and the traffic using it, by taking the high footpath on the right, which runs beside an attractive early-19th-century terrace of 18 houses called The Parade, and soon returns you to the Trafalgar roundabout and the car park.

AFTERWORD

"Plan for 90 acre Truro woodland" was the main headline in the 29 November 2001 issue of the *West Briton*. The owner of Park Farm, between Truro and Malpas, is proposing to develop a "community woodland", complete with a network of new footpaths linked to the existing rights of way. If this project goes ahead, with the benefit of funding (£90,000 - £100,000) expected from the Forestry Commission, it will greatly increase the options for those who want to shorten the walk route just described.

COUNTRY WALK 3 (SOUTH)
NEWHAM AND CALENICK
About four miles, plus a possible diversion of less than a mile.

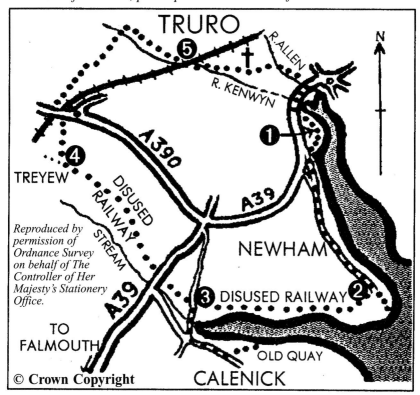

This is a walk of great contrasts, ranging from city-centre streets to Truro's answer to the Camel Trail. The footpath created from the former Newham Branch Line is of course much shorter than Padstow-to-Wenfordbridge, but it strongly rivals it for beauty, especially if you walk it during the winter months when there are no leaves on the trees to hide Calenick Creek; and in one respect it is better from the pedestrian's viewpoint: cyclists are not permitted to use the section north-west of Calenick, and although the rest is part of the National Cycle Network, at the time of writing it is comparatively little-used by cyclists.

It is an easy walk, mostly flat and on well-made tracks, minor roads and streets; the optional diversion at Calenick involves field-paths and therefore possibly mud underfoot. The ideal day for this walk would be a Sunday, when the streets of Truro are quiet and there is less if any of the heavy traffic which usually makes walking along the road beside the Truro River an uncomfortable experience. The only pubs, shops and public toilets on the route are in Truro.

Note: This is an updated version of a chapter originally published in *A Second View from Carn Marth*, now out of print. The focus in that book was on industrial history, and that topic is still prominent in what follows. Detailed information on other features is available in the City Centre Walkabout, Volumes 1 and 2, and several other books currently in print, such as the excellent series of large-format booklets produced by the Truro Buildings Research Group.

Directions are given from and back to the long-stay car park next to Tesco, beside the main by-pass road (A39, Morlaix Avenue - named after Truro's twin town in Brittany).

1 Go to the pavement beside the main road; turn right and right again immediately on to the riverside walk, which takes you along Garras Wharf.

TRURO AS A PORT

Just a couple of hundred yards behind you as you start to walk along Garras Wharf are Lemon Quay and Back Quay. They epitomise Truro's decline as a port: during the 1920s and '30s, after centuries of busy maritime activity, the river there was concreted over and turned into a car park. Of course, motor vehicles were just one factor among many that caused the change: bigger ships, silting and the growth of Falmouth were others. Records as far back as 1160 indicate Truro's importance in the exporting of tin and wool. In Tudor times, ships of 100 tons used Truro, and as the mining industry grew, so the port facilities expanded, with numerous quays and wharfs, often named after the men who had them built to serve their own businesses (Lemon, Enys and Worth are examples). Garras Wharf took its name from Garras silver-lead mine, just north of Idless, which had its own large smelting works here between about 1814 and 1850. The climax of shipping activity came in the 19th century, even though by then the silt excluded ships over 30 tons, and the cargoes from larger vessels had to be brought up from Malpas by barge. There was also a timber-yard, where rafts of imported timber were left in water to season. Despite the decline, Truro has never quite died as a port: a few cargo vessels (many bringing timber from Scandinavia) have continued to weave their way up the deep-water channels along with the pleasure-boats, and recently there has been some expansion of maritime business down-river at Newham.

On the top of the hill to your left is Truro School: see pages 74-5. The tall building bearing the letters HTP and the date 1911 was the flour mill built by

Hosken, Trevithick and Polkinhorne, a firm which later sold motor cars from showrooms at Back Quay. (See Volume 2 page 60.) **Continue beside the Truro River with Tesco's car park on your right at first, and then turn left along Newham Road. An attractive footway runs for some distance beside the Truro River; where that comes to an end you have, unfortunately, to negotiate a few hundred yards of the road itself, not much of which is provided with sidewalks. Please take great care, especially on weekdays, when there is likely to be heavy traffic, including large lorries.**

This photo was taken in 1988, when the "Newham Business Village" was under construction.

Newham, in Kea parish, was one of the four manors whose estates covered the area now occupied by Truro, the others being Trehaverne (Kenwyn parish), Moresk and Polwhele (both in St Clement parish). The "prestigious developments" of "Newham Business Village" on your right as you walk the riverside footway occupy the area where once stood Newham Station. The second building, clearly older than the rest, is actually a survival from the station: see the photograph on page 20 of Volume 2, and *The West Cornwall Railway* by S C Jenkins & R C Langley (Oakwood Press, 2002). The mansion on the hill above is Newham House, built by R.A.Daniell of Trelissick, who was appointed Sheriff of Cornwall in 1795 (see the later note on the Mansion House); from about 1891 to 1909 it housed the Old Truro Grammar School, which then became Truro Cathedral School and moved to the Cathedral Close. Also up on the right is the

GPO's sorting office, officially opened by Princess Diana early in 1991. Somewhere nearby must have stood the Newham Smelting Works; no-one seems to know its exact site.

NEWHAM SMELTING-HOUSE

Truro and its immediate surroundings were an important centre for tin-smelting. Up to the end of the 17th century, this was done in blowing-houses, in which bellows, driven by a water-wheel, raised the heat in the furnaces. In 1702, Robert Lydall took out a patent for a new technique using coal and anthracite instead of wood and charcoal, and dispensing with the bellows. The first use of the new "reverberatory furnace" in tin smelting was at Newham, where Lydall set up a smelting-house with ten such furnaces, in partnership with the aptly-named Francis Moult. The Newham works had several warehouses, a smithy, an office and other buildings, all surrounded by a high wall: secrecy was important - the workforce lived on the premises, and the manager kept firearms in his room. Blowing-house owners tried to prove that the new process produced inferior tin, but tests made by the Mint Office in 1708 found no significant difference. In 1711 the company built a new works at Calenick, apparently because of a lack of running water at Newham, and by about 1715 the Newham smelting-house had closed.

Looking up-river from Newham

Continue straight ahead. Take special care where the road narrows as it passes between the side-walls of a former railway-bridge. Go on past Little Newham house.

2 Turn right up Lighterage Hill (although you may care to make a short detour first by continuing ahead to look at the docks area). A few yards up Lighterage Hill, take the path on the left, where there is a National Cycle Network milepost. You are now on the track of the old Newham branch line.

THE NEWHAM BRANCH

In 1852 the West Cornwall Railway opened its line from Penzance to Truro; the original terminus was at Highertown, but in 1855 the line was extended to Newham. When the Cornwall Railway, linking Truro to Plymouth, built Truro Station in 1859, the West Cornwall trains were mostly diverted there, and the Newham section became a branch line, carrying only goods after 1863, but was not closed down until early November 1971, when a new freight depot opened at Truro Station.

After a short cutting in which the right-hand side has become a sort of natural rock-garden, you have trees on your left, with glimpses of Calenick Creek - an amazing contrast on a working day to the clanking cranes and Industrial Estate traffic a few hundred yards back. **After nearly a mile you reach a road.**

3 Turn left to visit Calenick village, which is attractive as well as historically important. The derivation of the name is uncertain, but it may mean "meadow" or "marshy place". The latter would be appropriate in view of the flooding which has plagued the village, especially in recent years, thanks partly to the rapid growth of Threemilestone and the western edge of Truro, causing increased run-off into the stream which flows into Calenick Creek. After a long delay, a flood-prevention scheme was finally put in place in 1998.

The clock tower of the old smelting house is on the right; unfortunately, the high wall makes for problems in seeing any of the other buildings, apart from the attractive slate-hung house, originally the manager's residence.

CALENICK SMELTING-HOUSE

In 1711, when the Calenick smelting-house was built, Calenick Creek was navigable at least as far as Magor's Quay (the one at the end of the diversion described later), so that coal could be delivered there. Silting increased rapidly after that, mainly because of slime coming from the Wheal Jane area: in 1877, for example, it is estimated that 10,000 tons was deposited in the creek and

Truro River from the Calenick stream alone. Even so, the smelting-house was the most successful of all the early ones in this area, and did not close down until 1891. In the yard was a workshop where crucibles were made, and pieces of these can still be found in the creek. They were used for assaying, testing the metallic content of the smelted ore.

COUNTRY WALK 3

On the left just before the bridge is the toll-house (this road was once the Falmouth-Truro turnpike!); notice, near the phone-box opposite, the Victorian post-box. Over the bridge, the first house on the right (River Cottage) was one of several pubs in Calenick in its industrial heyday; and beyond that is the former corn mill.

CALENICK MILL

A fulling mill stood here as early as 1300. Baptista Boazio's map of 1597 marks "The Mill" at "Carlinick". This was a grist mill serving the Manor of Newham. In April 1831 it was described as "newly built". It worked until about 1910, John Mutton being the last miller.

From here, either return straight away up the road to the path along the railway track, following the directions from point 4; or for a pleasant short diversion, turn left past the terraced cottages, known as Ropewalk Row for a reason that will emerge later. After a couple of hundred yards turn left between gate-posts (there is a wooden stile on the left of the gateway) into a field, then follow the line of the footpath diagonally right, to a gate at the edge of woodland. Continue through this till it brings you down to the creek - an attractive picnic-spot with a pretty view of the village. You also

Calenick from the old quay

see the salt-marsh through which the stream now winds; before the silting-up, caused largely by mining inland, the creek was tidal and navigable, as shown by the remains of quay walls at this point. In the small copse by the stream-bank just beyond the fence are a few hummocks and the base of an old wall: here once stood a limekiln. The open field beyond was once woodland, and through it ran the Rope Walk, which also extended into the wood beyond, where its course can still be made out. This is where ropes were spun, and it is said that several of the old ropes were found underneath the limekiln when it was demolished.

Return to the railway-track path by the same route and continue as before, now heading north-west. Soon on the right you pass a brick shed - one of two apparently used as stores for the railway. Below on the left, beside the embankment, you may be able to make out the course of the leat that once served the smelting works. By this point, the roar of traffic on the A39 will almost certainly have forced itself on your attention; soon a railway bridge takes you across that, and peace gradually returns, to match the tranquillity of the valley scenery. Somewhere down there flows the little River Tinny; perhaps easier to discern, at least in winter, is the spire of Kea Church among the trees on the far side of the valley. This is the second of two churches to have been built on that site in the 19th century, replacing the 15th century parish church at Old Kea. (See *Around the Fal*.) A little further along, the woodland closer at hand is Nansavallan ("apple-orchard valley") Wood. **About a mile past the first bridge is another crossing a country road near Treyew,** which was the site for another early tin-smelting operation, apparently closed down by 1770.

4 **Immediately after this, turn right, and then at the wider path turn left (that is, don't go down to the road you have just crossed on the bridge).** The path soon narrows and takes you round behind New County Hall. Towards the end look back for a good view - unless foliage obscures it - of Penweathers Junction, where the Falmouth Branch leaves the main London-Penzance line. **Unfortunately you now have to cross the main road - no easy matter, although a traffic island is conveniently placed to help. Continue ahead along Dobbs Lane.** In winter you may be able to make out the main line in the cutting on the right, then the railway station with Old County Hall just beyond. On the skyline further right is Sainsbury's supermarket, which occupies the former site of the Girls' Grammar School, once a well-known landmark. **The road curves downhill and becomes Bosvigo Lane**, which takes its name from the nearby Bosvigo House. The original house on that site probably dated from the 13th century; that was replaced in the 18th, and the new house was later acquired by the Lemon family of Carclew: see the later notes on the Mansion House and Princes House. The attractive garden of Bosvigo House is open to the public several days a week between early March and late September: ring 01872-275774 for details. (More information about Bosvigo is on page 101.)

As you reach the Kenwyn River you will see a road and path signposted to Coosebean on the left; Coosebean (Cornish, "little wood") was the site of yet another smelting house. Coosebean Mill is seen on Country Walk 4. **Cross the bridge and turn right along St George's Road, eventually passing under the railway viaduct.** Notice the stumps of Brunel's original structure on the far side. **Turn right** to inspect the old building currently occupied by the Steve Andrews tyre company, Trevails and other businesses, but apparently destined soon to be converted into residential accommodation. This was the Carvedras Smelting Works. If you go a few yards up the lane beside it and look into the yard on the right you will see it from the point where the photographer stood in 1893 when he took the picture reproduced in the drawing on page 22. (See tpages 17-22 for information about the smelting works, viaduct and other features on the next part of this route.)

5 Now return to the viaduct, cross St George's Road, and follow the sign to Victoria Gardens. Walk with the Kenwyn River on your left at first, then cross to the other side beside a sluice-gate. Now the river is on your right and a leat on your left; you are coming into the area known as The Leats. The leat powered a grist mill called Town Mills and a fulling-mill (for the scouring and cleaning of woollen cloth) owned by a Mr Tippet, whose name is preserved in a narrow passageway called Tippet's Backlet. More recently the leat supplied water flowing along the gutters in the city streets, an unusual feature which was described in 1865 as "conducing to the general salubrity of the town". At various times that flow has ceased as a result of a flood-prevention scheme up-river, or for other reasons such as vandalism and accidental blockages.

Continue along the path by the river, crossing (with great care because of fast traffic) Edward Street and Castle Street. When it is safe to do so, look up to the left at Edward Street to see the new Courts of Justice, built where Truro's cattle market used to be; long before that it was the probable site of the Norman castle. **After Castle Street, keep heading towards the Cathedral.** The river and leat are now underground, and it is this area and especially Victoria Square beyond that was particularly badly hit by flooding in 1988. **Leading both right and left are several narrow passageways**, known in Truro as "opways" or "ops"(despite the spelling usually seen, "opes"). **Turn left on any one of them, and you will soon reach High Cross, overshadowed by the west**

end of the Cathedral. Turn left along the street on the south side of the Cathedral, right into Cathedral Lane, and left at the main street, named Boscawen Street. The Victorian "Gothick" building at the end stands on the site of the old Coinage Hall. In recent years it was the Trustee Savings Bank; it currently serves as a pizza parlour, with a Victorian-style tearoom on the upper floor from which a fine panorama of Boscawen Street can be seen.

THE COINAGE HALL

Since the 14th century Truro had been one of the coinage towns. Twice a year, officials from London came to the Coinage Hall to test the quality of tin ingots by striking off a corner or "coign"; duty was levied, which went to the Duchy of Cornwall; the tin was then marked by the coinage-hammer and could be sold - although much tin was smuggled out of the county untaxed. "At coinage time in Truro and Penzance," writes B. Trevail, "huge blocks of tin, too heavy to be stolen, littered all the principal streets, with pack animals and carriers' carts coming and going from the coinage hall and the surrounding smelting houses."
On the upper floor of the Coinage Hall regular Stannary Courts were held, and occasional Stannary Parliaments (Latin, stannum, tin). The rights of the tinners to govern their own affairs date back to 1197 and have been jealously guarded in Cornwall; the Parliament, meeting then at its oldest seat, Lostwithiel, created a stir as lately as 1974 by making an official protest to the Soviet Ambassador about Russian fishing boats "poaching" Cornish fish stocks. In the same year the Parliament approved the issue of special Cornish banknotes - including notes for five and ten shillings, since the Stannary Parliament had never sanctioned decimalisation! More recently, an attempt to use Stannary laws as a means of avoiding payment of Poll Tax received much publicity.

Walk up to this and take the right fork, Princes Street, where you will now pass the Mansion House and Princes House on the right, and on the left just before the by-pass road, the Old Mansion House.

TRURO'S GRAND 18th-CENTURY HOUSES

The Mansion House was built about 1760 by the London architect Thomas Edwards, using Bath stone for most of the frontage, for Thomas Daniell. Daniell had been chief clerk to Sir William Lemon (see the next paragraph); partly because of marrying into money, he was able to buy up the Lemon mining interests on Sir William's death. His son, Ralph Allen Daniell, was nicknamed "Guinea-a-minute" because this was said to have been his income from one mine alone.

The house once had a garden leading down to Back Quay on the River Kenwyn; part of it is now "Tinners Yard".

Princes House was designed about twenty years earlier by the same architect for William Lemon. Notice the rather more decorative style that was in fashion then. The entrance steps and porch, designed by Silvanus Trevail, were added in 1893. Inside, there are fine balustrades and fireplaces and much magnificent plasterwork. Born in 1696, William Lemon as a young man became manager of a smelting works. In the 1720s one of his mines was among the first to use Newcomen's steam pumping engine in Cornwall. The bulk of his fortune was made from copper mining, and at his death he left £300,000 - a vast sum when translated into modern values. His country home was Carclew, overlooking Devoran and Restronguet Creek; enlargements to this, too, were designed for him by Thomas Edwards.

The Old Mansion House was the town house of Samuel Enys, and seems to have been built between 1706 and 1713 - so each of these three great houses in turn takes us a little further back in time. Enys inherited a large sum from his grandfather; with it he bought the Manor of Kenwyn and Truro, and also a large number of shares in mines and smelting-houses. (Incidentally, the grandfather just mentioned was Henry Gregor, whose family built "The Great House", later called Blackford's, on the corner next to Princes House. This is the oldest of all Truro's grand houses, but it was badly damaged by fire in 1923. Extensive renovation has been carried out in recent years.)

Walk back a few yards and take the right fork (Quay Street), back towards the Cathedral, then right into New Bridge Street. Immediately after crossing the bridge over the River Allen, turn right, under the archway of Highshore House, to walk by the river, with Enys Quay on the opposite side. On the left, where there are now modern residential apartments, used to stand the factory buildings used by Furniss's, manufacturers of sweets and biscuits (see page 51); "Furniss Island", which you are now on, is said to have been created by centuries of garbage. **At the main road use the subway, and on the far side turn right, crossing both the rivers and returning to the car park.**

COUNTRY WALK 4 (WEST)
COOSEBEAN, NEW MILL AND TREWORDER
About 4° miles - or you could leave out Treworder
and shorten the walk to about 3 miles.

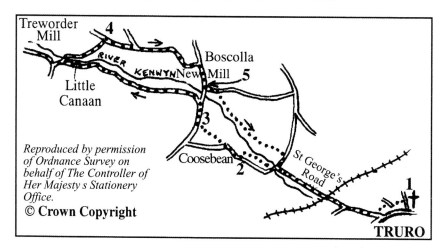

Treworder Mill **4**

Boscolla

RIVER KENWYN New Mill **5**

Little Canaan

3

Reproduced by permission of Ordnance Survey on behalf of The Controller of Her Majesty's Stationery Office.
© Crown Copyright

Coosebean **2**

St George's Road

1

TRURO

This walk explores the lovely Kenwyn Valley - peaceful, sheltered and full of the sounds of water. In this charmed spot it's hard to believe that the busy city traffic is within a mile or two. You will see several old mills, all now beautifully converted into houses, and there are superb views of Truro and rolling countryside. When my wife and I last did it, in April 2002, there were masses of celandines, bluebells and wild garlic (three-cornered leek), and the gorse was intermingled with swathes of brilliant white blackthorn, along with the blossom of apple, plum and cherry trees. Most of the walk is on quiet little roads, offering no problems to walkers apart from a few hills. The footpath beside the river from New Mill back to Truro involves climbing eight stiles, a few of which you (and/or your dog if you plan to take him or her along) might find difficult; the easiest way to avoid these would be to retrace your steps along the route by which you originally left the city. Waterproof footwear would be best, although all was dry underfoot when I last walked this route.

1 From the cathedral go to Pydar Street and through to The Leats via Pydar Mews or any of the other "opes", and then to River Street via another such passageway. Turn right up River Street and continue along Frances Street and St George's Road. Information about points of interest in River Street and Frances Street, and about St George's Chapel and Church is included in section 3 of the City Centre Walkabout. Beside the modern viaduct are the stumps of Brunel's original structure. (See my comments on the viaduct at Daubuz's Moors, on page 71.) The River Kenwyn is on your left as you continue up St George's Road. **Turn left over the bridge at Bosvigo Lane** (see the note about Bosvigo House on page 101)**, but don't go up on the raised path,because now you have to cross the road and take the signposted footpath which runs along the southern bank of the river.** Once there were many watermills along the Kenwyn; relics of a leat are near the path. **After crossing two stiles you reach Coosebean or Goosebean ("little wood") Mill. Here turn left.**

COOSEBEAN MILL

This is the last mill on the Kenwyn River to retain relics of its workings as a flour mill. (All the other mills upstream, including New Mill, Treworder, Polmooth, Tregavethan and Boscolleth, appear to have ceased work before the end of the 19th century, to be replaced by Coosebean with its greater power resources, greater capacity, better processing techniques and better transport facilities.) The wide cast-iron and wood overshot waterwheel and external driving gear, together with four millstones, may still be seen outside the building, now converted into three flats.

Coosebean Mill, 2002 (Photograph by Anthony Hitchens Unwin)

In 1777 it was described as "Coosebean melting and blowing house, in full working and perfect repair, with six melting furnaces and a complete blowing-house, the whole quite new-built." (A blowing house was an early form of tin-smelting house, fuelled by charcoal. The temperature in the furnace was raised by bellows driven by a waterwheel.) In 1794 there was a paper mill at Coosebean, and by 1804 a grist mill had been added. The melting house / blowing house had closed by 1810. In 1827 the paper mill - described by then as "one of the largest paper manufactories in the west of England and employing forty" - was completely destroyed by fire. It was rebuilt with the insurance money and, despite a second, smaller fire in 1834, it continued producing paper till 1836. Finally, after some twenty years lying idle it was converted as a flour mill with five pairs of stones, two waterwheels and a 20-horsepower engine. It had ceased working by 1926.

The surviving wheel here is very finely constructed and powerful, 14 feet by 6 feet, with 8 pairs of timber arms and 40 timber buckets. It is one of the widest wheels left in Cornwall.

2 Turn right on the road. You soon cross a stream; notice the mill leat culverted under the road beside the stream. The sluice gates are gone now. The name of the house "The Mowhay", on the right next, refers to a paddock close to a farmhouse. It is said (in Cornwall at least) to rhyme with "cowy", if such a word existed!

After about a quarter of a mile take the footpath on the right, signed to Treliske Lane. Walk near the hedge on your left (look back for a deservedly famous view of Truro).

Truro from the path near Treliske Lane

COUNTRY WALK 4

When you come to a gap in the field boundaries, go down a little way to the right, cross the granite stile and follow the sunken track from there. (If, however, this is too boggy underfoot, you can follow the example of many other walkers and keep to the edge of the field above.)

A second granite stile brings you to a road.

3 At the road turn right, towards New Mill.

NEW MILL

This mill is recorded in 1366 as Melynnewyth juxta Hendra, and in 1439 the miller or "Milward" was Peter of Melynnewyth, a Breton. (Bretons were frequently to be found in such occupations, being considered too lazy for anything else!) When advertised to let in 1841 it was said to be "erected about 12 months since on the most approved principles". The last recorded miller was Thomas Harris in 1856, but the mill may have been used by farmers after that date.

The waterwheel was behind the modern conversion, where a recently built extension now stands. The lane to Treworder follows the course of the long leat, interrupted about half-way along by an old pump-house, which made use of the older leat.

At New Mill

COUNTRY WALK 4

To shorten the walk, cross the river and take the first right turning, following the directions from point 5, line 3 ... unless, of course, the difficult stiles are too much of a deterrent.

To continue to Treworder, just before the old mill tail race and ford turn left and follow this pretty valley road for the best part of a mile. Soon on your right you have quite a good view, over a double gate, of the flood control work that has been carried out in recent years. (The work was completed in 1991.) The river is culverted beneath a dam. Further along, notice the old leat, now dry, between the road and the river.

You could turn right at Little Canaan Farm or the bridge a little way beyond, but first it's worth going just a short way further to look at Treworder Mill, very attractively converted and set in superb gardens.

TREWORDER MILL

The mill building, now gone, adjoined the mill cottage where a large annexe now stands. It served the manor of Treworder, together with Polmooth Mill and blowing house not far away. Both are mentioned in a document of 1612. When the manor of Treworder was for sale in June 1848, Treworder Mill tenement consisted of "good Dwelling House, new and capital Grist Mill, lately re-built at considerable expense, 22 acres of Arable and Meadow Land, well-stocked orchards, now in the occupation of Mr William Rosewarne as tenant." In 1853 the mill was described as "double", meaning that it had two pairs of stones. The last mention of the mill, in Kelly's Directory of 1856, names William Rosewarne as "miller and farmer", but like New Mill it may have continued working later than that.

Now return to the bridge just mentioned and fork left to cross it. Soon you pass Little Canaan, another idyllic spot with its ford and footbridge. (Cornwall has quite a few Biblical place-names, such as Salem and Jericho Valley; many of them were inspired by the religious fervour created by John Wesley.) **Continue up the quite steep hill.**

4 At the T-Junction turn right. After the footbridge by the ford, keep straight on at the road junction, past Ninnis Farm (from Cornish *enys,* island; in this case it probably means "river meadow"). On the skyline to the right is the Royal Cornwall Hospital, Treliske, with the independent Duchy Hospital to the right of it. **Continue through the small group of houses at Boscolla and down the hill to New Mill.**

5 Continue over the footbridge if you prefer to avoid the stiles I mentioned

earlier, and return to Truro by the way you came; but for the riverside path, turn left before the ford and take the footpath which starts with two rickety stiles beside a building on the right. The path beyond them keeps quite close to the river at first (though in wet weather you may need to go a little higher). Eventually it climbs away from the river, passing under two sets of power lines (it's a pity that the electricity cables are so prominent in this attractive, wide valley), and at this stage you get a view to the right which takes in the long, low roof of the railway station, Old County Hall further right, and Sainsbury's beyond that. **After one last stile close to houses, go along a short lane and turn right at the road.** This is Comprigney Hill, apparently meaning "gallows hill" (from Cornish *cloghprennyer,* literally "bellbeams"). **Turn left into St George's Road** (see below *)**, and from here you can retrace your earlier footsteps to return to the cathedral. Immediately after passing beneath the railway viaduct you might prefer to take the path on the left that runs between the Kenwyn River and the leat rather than continuing along St George's Road, Frances Street and River Street.**

* As you reach St George's Road you are again close to Bosvigo House, whose very attractive three-acre gardens are often open to the public. (The latest information I have is that opening times are from 11am to 6 pm every Wednesday, Thursday, Friday and Saturday between early March and late September; for up-to-date details including admission charges, phone 01872 275774.) The house (name pronounced "Bos-**vie**-go", the middle syllable rhyming with "eye") dates at least from the early 18th century but was greatly altered in more recent times. There is a well-stocked Victorian conservatory, a series of walled gardens and a sloping, wooded area with walks "among many unusual plants," as Douglas Ellory Pett says. "Bosvigo," he adds, "is exceptional in Cornwall for its range of herbaceous plants, and for their associations." "A plantsman's garden best in summer," say the owners, Wendy and Michael Perry.

Bibliography
(supplementary to the Bibliographies in Volumes 1 & 2)

Acton, Bob, *Around the Fal*, Landfall Publications, 2003 (updated version, includes directions and historical details of walks near Truro, visiting such places as Cowlands, Coombe, Devoran, Point, Penpol, Feock, Trelissick, Ruan Lanihorne, St Just and St Mawes)

Ferris, Andrew, "A Brief History of (Our) Time", article on the Ferris family, *Restronguet Creek Society Newsletter* 2003 (Includes several paragraphs about the family's contribution to the Truro scene)

Fogg, Roger, *Pencalenick, A History in words and pictures*, Packet Publishing 1998

Jenkins, S.C. & Langley, R.C., *The West Cornwall Railway, Truro to Penzance*, Oakwood Press, 2002

Park, Jo, *The Church of St John the Evangelist, Truro,* published by the author, 1984

Parnell, Christine, *Truro, History & Guide*, Tempus Publishing, 2002

The March for Cornwall passes the Lander Monument at the top of Lemon Street, May 1977

Viv Acton
A HISTORY OF TRURO
Volume 1: From Coinage Town to Cathedral City

"...this rivetting publication" (Colin Gregory, *Western Morning News*)

"... stimulating reading and a fascinating look into the past" (Jill Richards, *Cornwall Now*)

"The stories of Truro's hunger, festivals, fires and floods all contribute to an excellent book packed with information and presented in a delightful manner. This is an important book." (Phil Hosken, *Cornish World*)

"... a valuable addition to the bibliography of Cornish town histories." (Dr James Whetter, *Cornish Banner*)

"This is a book which is going to be a classic." (Joan Rendell, *Old Cornwall*)

"If you not only like to read about local history but are consumed by it, then this book is a must." (Alison Cock, *West Briton*)

Hardback, £12.00   Paperback, £8.25

Viv & Bob Acton
A HISTORY OF TRURO
Volume 2: Cathedral City and County Town

"So, you think you know Truro? Delve into Volume 2 of *A History of Truro* by Bob and the late Viv Acton, and you'll quickly learn just how little you know - or had forgotten. ... Of just under 300 pages, this is an eminently readable chronicle of the evolution of Truro from 1880 to 2002." (Shirley Salmon, *West Briton*)

"... a valuable document of Truro's social history and development" (*Cornish World*)

"Mr Acton has produced a fine book of (Truro's) recent history." (Dr James Whetter, *Cornish Banner*)

"Full marks to Bob Acton for taking on this work. Readers will not be disappointed by what they find. Volume three is eagerly awaited." (Stephen Ivall, *Falmouth Packet*)

"This is a valuable book which must be read by all who have Truro's and Cornwall's interests at heart." (Donald Rawe, *Western Morning News*)

"I would recommend this book to all who have a love for and an interest in Truro and to all those who have fond memories of Viv." (June Palmer, *Journal of the Cornwall Association of Local Historians*)

"I have enjoyed this 'Truro learning curve', and so will you." (John Neale, *Old Cornwall*)

Paperback, £9.99

103

MORE LANDFALL BOOKS

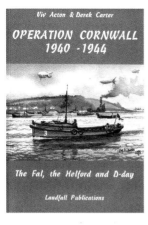

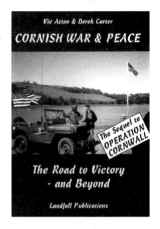

These two very popular books tell the story of Cornwall during World War 2. They focus, though not exclusively, on the Fal and Helford areas.

Price £6.99 each

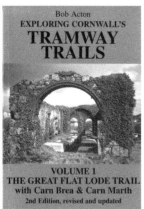

These two books are detailed, fully illustrated guides to the Mineral Tramways Project routes (for walkers, cyclists and equestrians) between Portreath and Devoran and around Carn Brea.

Price £7.50 each

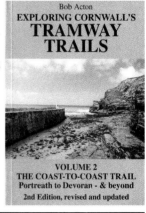

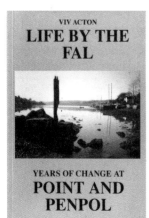

A history of this interesting district beside Restronguet Creek, once highly industrialised.

Price £4.95